I0760168

Exploring a new era – hybrid, blended and online learning

Greg Whateley, Andrew West and Ashok Chanda

(With a foreword by Angus Hooke)

First Published in 2021 by 1visionOT Pty Ltd trading as Smart Questions, Suite 3, 596 North Road, Ormond, VIC 3204, Australia

Web: *www.smart-questions.com* (including ordering of printed and electronic copies, extended book information and community contributions)

Email: *info@smart-questions.com* (for customer services, bulk order enquiries, reproduction requests et al)

A catalogue record for this book is available from the British Library.

ISBN 978-1-907453-31-1

SQ-23-202-001-001

Table of Contents

SECTION 2 – THE RESPONSE

Foreword

Universal Business School Sydney (UBSS) is a private business school that delivers undergraduate and postgraduate degrees in Business, Entrepreneurship and IT/Cyber Studies to domestic and international students. It is developing a rapidly growing reputation for providing very high-quality content and using state-of-the art delivery modes. These have resulted in high levels of student satisfaction. According to data collected by Quality Indicators for Learning and Teaching (QILT), the tool used by DET to monitor student satisfaction in higher education in Australia, the School received an average student satisfaction score of 80.8% in 2018-20, compared with 77.4% recorded by Sydney's four public universities. In 2020, reflecting mainly the effects of the COVID-19 transition to online learning, the average score in the four public universities fell to 69.2%. However, at UBBS, student satisfaction increased to 81.2% tripling the gap with the four public universities, to 12 percentage points.

The widening gap in student satisfaction can be attributed to the speed and effectiveness with which UBSS adjusted to the need to move to online learning. Its academic team, led by Emeritus Professor Greg Whateley, Professor Andrew West, and Associate Professor Ashok Chanda, had been working for about a year on a hybrid model that would include quality onsite delivery while providing students with the choice of onsite or offsite access to this delivery. By investing in TED-type lecture theatres equipped with tracking cameras, very high-quality audio, clear graphics, and appropriate lighting, and by requiring lecturers to deliver their material onsite in professional dress code and style, UBSS was able within a few weeks to deliver engaging classes to its students online. The transition was so successful that, in a survey in mid-2021, 92% of students reported not only that they were happy with the new mode of delivery, but that they would like to complete their degrees online.

This book contains the personal stories of management, marketing, administration, and academic staff as they made the forced move from face-to-face to online delivery, how they view the new delivery mode about 18 months later, and how they believe that education delivery can and should change in the coming years. It is essential reading for all persons working in the higher education industry or just interested in how we can continue to provide quality education to domestic and overseas students in this rapidly changing world.

Professor Angus Hooke

UBSS Centre for Scholarship and Research

Preface

This publication began with three stimulus papers on *hybrid learning* (Whateley), *blended learning* (West) and *online learning* (Chanda). The three papers (now Section 1 of this book) in turn were presented to selected authors for consideration and response.

Sixteen responses were received and are used as the additional chapters (now Section 2 of this book) and provide a valuable insight into the impact of COVID-19 on current practices in a diverse range of higher education settings and foci. The chapters also represent projections on what the future of delivery and management in the sector will look like going forward.

Ian Bofinger (Chapter 4) relates the creation of The Virtual Conservatorium in 2004 and notes that the principles outlined in the initiative are now the very same principles applied to managing higher education music today given the restrictions placed on organisation by the pandemic.

Anurag Kanwar (Chapter 5) delves into the organisational challenge imposed by online learning including IT, staff training and the regulatory environment.

Greg Whateley (Chapter 6) explores the variety of options (alternate delivery) that have developed over a number of years are now most relevant to higher education – and particularly international student education.

Ashok Chanda (Chapter 7) outlines the all-important aspect of digitalising content in this current context.

Jim Mienczakowski (Chapter 8) discusses the notion that higher education students may no longer go to university as such – as the experience is replaced by a range of options that may just as effectively provide a most satisfactory student experience.

Rhonda Rowland (Chapter 9) energises an understanding of the needs of international students and the impact that the pandemic and the reliance on eLearning has had on learning and life.

Anurag Kanwar (Chapter 10) provides useful guidelines on what you need to know about online learning and subsequently teaching online.

Cyril Jankoff (Chapter 11) speaks to the topic of blended learning for executive students and relates his own personal teaching experiences.

Art Phillips (Chapter 12) highlights additional supporting options such as guest interviews online that can significantly contribute to student engagement.

Tom O'Connor (Chapter 13) provides a most valuable insight into the teaching on the VCS in China via the use of technology.

Jotsana Roopram (Chapter 14) explores the issue of online assessment in the new digital world.

Sam Sorace (Chapter 15) reflects on being a mature aged postgraduate student in the blended learning environment.

Lauren Whateley (Chapter 16) considers the issues associated with being an online student.

Andy Wong (Chapter 17) outlines the approach to blended learning adopted and expanded within the higher education music context in Singapore.

Richard Xi (Chapter 18) details the considerations necessary to cater for international postgraduate students in the blended learning environment.

Stephen JK Parker (Chapter 19) discusses ways to address the question "are the there?" when delivering online lectures.

The authors wish to thank sincerely the responders for their invaluable insights and the fact that all chapters were produced within 30 days of initial contact. The speed has ensured the relevance and currency of the issues considered. We would also like to take the opportunity of thanking **Veronica Sorace, Angus Hooke** and **Stephen Parker** for their efforts and support.

Our view is that the conditions and circumstances resulting from the COVID-19 pandemic have changed the thinking around hybrid, blended and online learning and many of these responses will remain with the sector for some time.

Greg Whateley, Andrew West, Ashok Chanda

UBSS Centre for Scholarship and Research, September 2021

Section 1:

The Stimulus Papers

Chapter

1

What is meant by 'hybrid' delivery and how does it work in higher education?

Greg Whateley

INTRODUCTION

There appears to be some confusion in the sector around the meaning and application of 'hybrid' delivery to higher education students. The misleading (and incorrect) view is that teaching students online while also providing a face-to-face classroom option requires two sets of activities. In fact, 'hybrid' delivery is a simultaneous activity requiring no more preparation or time than F2F teaching. What is does require, however, is a commitment to excellence.

The Toyota Kluger Hybrid[1] lays out the foundations for the concept. It is one car with two options. The driver decides which mode to use, and this can be altered, as required, along the journey. Using the analogy, then, in the context of higher education and the delivery of teaching and learning within the context, teaching would be available in both modes simultaneously (online and F2F) and the student would decide on the mode – and this could be altered along the journey.

[1] *www.toyota.com.au/Kluger*

HYBRID HIGHER EDUCATION

Barnes (2021)[2] has missed the point, and in a recent article has somehow constructed a model of teaching twice - first online, then F2F - effectively, doubling the effort. Zhou and Tariq (2021)[3] suggested that, although the hybrid practice requires effort, it is not a duplication of activity and there is certainly no 'doubling up'. In reality, it is a single (demanding) task delivered in a dual mode. The model is well described on the Monash University site[4]. The student chooses the mode that best suits them and their circumstances. This can vary from subject to subject, and, in fact, from week to week, that is, one week a student may view the course online and the following week decide to step on campus for a F2F experience – this may continue throughout a trimester as the student best sees fit. The real issue will lie in the capacity of the campus management to always ensure a COVID safe environment. A range of protocols is already in place in order to minimise exposure and maintain a very high level of hygiene.

Basically, a well set up classroom - with elements of a TV studio added - provides the perfect location and vehicle for hybrid delivery. The more theoretical the subject, the easier the task. Practical classes, however, come with certain challenges. These challenges may require a physical presence on campus – whether for a full trimester at a time will be determined by the nature of the practical. If the session is practical/observation based, then the hybrid model works well. This will vary from course to course and from institution to institution. In my institution – a business school – the hybrid model is ideal.

REQUIREMENTS

There are, however, certain requirements for delivering the hybrid mode and these will demand both careful consideration (from the outset) and capital investment (from the outset and along the way).

---

[2] *https://www.theguardian.com/australia-news/2021/jun/20/universities-ramping-up-hybrid-learning-means-double-the-work-for-same-pay-staff-say*

[3] *https://blog.highereducationwhisperer.com/2021/06/teaching-hybrid-mode-in-dual-delivery.html*

[4] *https://www.monash.edu/learning-teaching/teaching-resources/search/user-guides/hybrid-teaching-models*

First, the activity needs to take place on campus, irrespective of the number of students wishing to physically attend the session. The lecturer / presenter in situ then provides the option of teaching a fully online class, or alternatively (and simultaneously), the option to sit in class in a COVID-19 safe manner - not unlike a live television audience. My institution refers to such classes as TEDx-style presentations[5]. The 'live audience' option fulfils the criteria for a 'hybrid' approach. The model requires a well-equipped and maintained studio environment with designated seating locations for the students when on site.

Second, there are certain IT requirements if one is to ensure the quality of the delivery, including *picture* (ideally a tracking camera), *audio* (essential) and supporting *slides / graphics.* The look and feel of the presentations must be impressive, from the outset, and this will require appropriate *lighting* and *dress code.* Essentially, we need to be aiming for TV quality output. The special emphasis needs to be on audio – which is usually the tell-tale sign of poor production. This, no doubt, puts pressure on the presenter from the outset. Teaching needs to be informed, efficient and entertaining - the requirements of good teaching anyway. There is little room for low-end presentations with tedious disruptions and poor audio graphics. The model requires a professional approach with appropriate IT support and maintenance.

Third, the lecturer / presenter needs to remain aware that it is a 'live' presentation, and so, is required to commit to a dynamic (dare I say, entertaining) performance. Shuffling through notes, head down, coughing, grumbling and repetition, are unacceptable. These events need to be focused and dynamic; they need to be well prepared, and seamlessly presented. A live audience can sometimes enhance the presentation with appropriate responses, but essentially, the presenter needs to be 'mindful' that many students are online.

Finally, hybrid education is not about recording a presentation and reusing it in subsequent trimesters / semesters. Recordings are valuable revision resources for students, but nothing can (nor should) replace live sessions, albeit online or F2F. This is not about cost cutting and time saving - it is about a quality, multiple mode delivery. The temptation for a number of institutions has been to

---

[5] *https://www.ted.com/watch/tedx-talks*

record once – and deliver the same product over multiple trimesters –and this has been heavily criticised by students (as demonstrated in the 2020 QILT outcomes) who, in turn, find it difficult to reconcile the presentation standard with the fees charged. Delivering from home (as opposed to on campus in well-equipped studios) has had a significant impact on quality and has contributed to high levels of student dissatisfaction. The student experience is not necessarily diminished using the hybrid option.

FUTURE OF HYBRID

There is little doubt that hybrid (in its true sense) will be with us for some time. It is predicted that 2021 and 2022 will be a hybrid period but elements of the concept will remain in the long term[6]. Busteed (2021) is of the same opinion.[7]

It will come as no surprise that many students (both international and domestic) onshore in Australia will choose online delivery as well as F2F. In a recent survey of students at my own institution[8], 92% expressed the current desire to stay online, even in place of a hybrid option. It is likely that students will wish to return to some form of F2F throughout 2022, but it is also highly likely that students will want to maintain the option of mode choice – 'hybrid', moving forward.

The hybrid model of delivery affords higher education providers a genuine quality option that can be delivered effectively and efficiently, and certainly, without the double effort mistakenly proposed by some. Hybrid is not a shortcut though; it is an attempt at a quality outcome, given the extraordinary circumstances in which we find ourselves embedded. It also offers far reaching opportunities for students who, for whatever reason, find access to provider facilities difficult.

Emeritus Professor Greg Whateley, Deputy Vice Chancellor, Group Colleges Australia

[6] *https://www.campusreview.com.au/2021/06/what-the-lack-of-onshore-international-students-in-2021-means-for-2022/*

[7] *https://www.forbes.com/sites/brandonbusteed/2021/05/02/pandemic-to-permanent-11-lasting-changes-to-higher-education/?sh=137189bb452f*

[8] *https://www.ubss.edu.au/*

Chapter

2

What is meant by 'blended' delivery and how does it work in higher education?

Andrew West

INTRODUCTION

This chapter will explore the distinctive characteristics of Blended Learning (bL), how it complements other modes of delivery and replicates the modern workplace.

As outlined in Chapter 1 by Emeritus Professor Whateley, "hybrid delivery is a simultaneous activity requiring no more preparation or time than F2F teaching…teaching would be available in both modes simultaneously (online and F2F) and the student would decide on the mode – and this could be altered along the journey." Hybrid delivery is therefore synchronous, allowing the student the opportunity to choose their mode or switch between the two, depending on their preference during the individual unit or the whole program.

Chapter 3, by Associate Professor Chanda, provides details pertaining to online, where delivery is fully online, incorporating no F2F. Blended Learning is a mix of both online and F2F, not simultaneous, with the mode of delivery determined by the designer and lecturer, to maximise pedagogical and curriculum outcomes for the student.

BLENDED LEARNING FRAMEWORK AND PRACTICAL APPLICATION OVER TIME

The term Blended Learning (bL) has been used in the education sphere since the 1960s when computers and information technology were first making an impact on all levels of education, however, it was not until the early 2000s that definitional and conceptual research into bL started to take hold. This initial research can be divided into three main foci. There is the emphasis on the delivery media or how the instructional modalities are combined[9]. Second, there is a focus on the combination of the methods and curriculum design as a form of bL[10]. The third area of focus is the instruction and how this is combined across online and F2F[11].

It was not until 2006, with Bonk and Graham's[12] Handbook of Blended Learning, that the term became more clearly defined and a framework for its use was explored. Bonk and Graham took the term bL, which had been applied to a wide variety of pedagogies and technologies in a range of combinations, and provided a framework for the term, their definition being "blended learning systems" as learning systems that "combine face-to-face (F2F) instruction with computer mediated instruction."[13]

BLENDED LEARNING ACCELERATED BY WEB 2.0

The growth in the practical application of bL coincides with developments in digital technologies, namely Web 2.0. The first of

[9] Orey, M (2002). One year of online blended learning: Lessons learned. Paper presented at the Annual Meeting of the Eastern Educational Research Association, Sarasota, FL

[10] Driscoll, M (2002). Blended Learning: Let's get beyond the hype. eLearning, 54.

[11] Reay, J (2001). Blended Learning - a fusion for the future. Knowledge Management Review, 4(3), 6.

[12] Bonk, C and Graham, C (Eds.). (2006). Handbook of Blended Learning: Global Perspectives, Local Designs. San Francisco, CA: Pfeiffer Publishing.

[13] Bonk, C and Graham, C (Eds.). (2006). Handbook of Blended Learning: Global Perspectives, Local Designs. San Francisco, CA: Pfeiffer Publishing.

the Web 2.0 recognised platforms emerged during 2004-2006. Web 2.0 enables users to collaborate and interact with the provider and with each other through social media as authors of their own user generated content that is shared in virtual communities. Prior to Web 2.0, viewers of web content were limited to viewing the content in a passive manner, with no interaction.

Many of these Web 2.0 sites and features are common today and include social media sites, Facebook, Instagram, YouTube, Redditt, all of which use Web 2.0 computer language and attributes. These allow user generated content through blogs, wikis, tagging keywords, likes, shares, hosted services, web applications (apps) and mashup applications.

Consumer evaluation and opinion sites, such as, Amazon, eBay, and TripAdvisor, are all built on Web 2.0. News and media have been changed forever through comments and shares on news sites. Twitter has also allowed political and industry voices to bypass traditional media to go straight to their constituents without editorial oversight and filtering to great effect.

These Web 2.0 features are applied in bL to allow the full richness of collaborative learning to occur, where there is a move away from didactic chalk and talk instruction from the master lecturer to servant students. There is a more collaborative shared learning and understanding of a topic approach, with the teacher becoming more of a facilitator and enabler of knowledge.

With the use of Web2.0, the education experience is heightened. The characteristics of Web 2.0 used in the media and consumer facets of society equally apply to education.

BLENDED LEARNING MODELS

As blended learning has developed over the last 15 years, distinct models of bL have emerged. By understanding these different models, bL pedagogy and learning design is maximised. The diagram below provides a framework for how F2F bricks and mortar learning blended with online learning has led to four models[14]. The four models are on a continuum, from the rotation model that is the most F2F focussed through to the enriched virtual model which has the highest level of online learning.

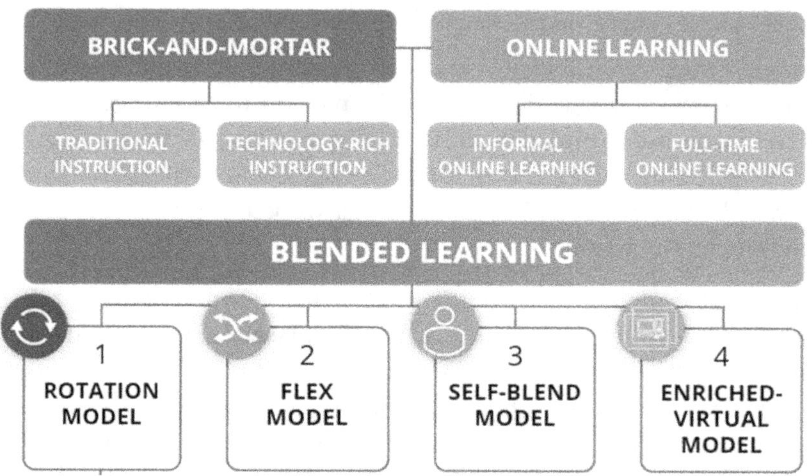

1. **Rotation Model**: students rotate between different learning activities within a single class, where at least one of the activities is completed online. Some examples of these rotation activities may include instructor-led sessions, group activities, one-on-one with the instructor and independent study time. In this form of bL, students learn mostly F2F with the instructor, and most of the time is spent F2F.
2. For the **Flex Model**, students primarily learn in F2F mode, but the foundational work is done online. Online activities are available both before and after the F2F instruction. This allows students to learn at their own pace online, working through a structured curriculum that underpins the F2F learning. When students are in F2F mode, the instructor focuses on the more challenging aspects of the curriculum, allowing time to focus on particular topics and go deeper to enrich the learning related to selected topics. The instructor becomes a facilitator, with the F2F learning time spent in small group activities, and/or with an emphasis on project

[14] Horn, M and Staker. H (2014) Blended: Using Disruptive Innovation to Improve Schools. San Francisco, CA: Jossey-Bass, 2014.

and case study based learning and one-on-one instructional support.

3. The **Self-Blend Model** allows students to choose the modules or micro courses to take online to supplement the F2F instruction. These modules are often taken from a structured curriculum, with elective topics on offer within a subject or elective subjects within a course. Constructive alignment and designed assessment of the modules ensures that all course level learning outcomes are met.
4. In the **Enriched Virtual Model**, the student spends most of their time online, with minimal guidance and F2F time from the instructor. This is different to the fully online study mode, as there is still a component of F2F, where meeting instructors on a regular basis and experiencing campus life with students joining their peers to discuss and network F2F, are features.

At UBSS, the **Flex Model** is applied in the Executive Delivery MBA program. During most of the study period, students participate in self-directed, structured online learning. Once this base knowledge has been achieved, they come together for a block intensive with other students and the lecturer who guides the intense deep learning of the material. This promotes a collaborative and shared learning experience for the students. The F2F room design is cabaret style desk placement to promote interaction between students. This enables them to share their life learned experience, to contextualise and embed the theories and concepts of the curriculum.

BLENDED LEARNING REPLICATES THE POST COVID WORKPLACE

In recent times, there is more of a focus on higher education graduate capabilities with regard to the behaviours, attributes and attitudes students require to work in today's organisations. These include digital literacy, remote work, virtual teamwork and collaboration, virtual project management, time management, goal orientation, to name a few. For recruiters taking on new employees and human resource departments evaluating promotion, these are the workplace attributes they look for in candidates.

COVID-19 has been an accelerator of social and technological trends. One of these is the move to virtual work, working from home and a hybrid model of some remote work and some time in the workplace. It is estimated that 56% of work undertaken in developed economies can be completed partially at home[15]. This increases significantly for digital, management and professional services work, and is most pronounced in IT based companies, where many global tech giants have announced a new workplace policy of Work from Anywhere (WFA). Spotify, with 6,500 employees across 73 countries, has a WFA policy. This is also the case for Atlassian, Salesforce and Dropbox[16]. As more of the workforce is tech based, and traditional industries embed more digital literate employees, this trend will continue after the impact of COVID-19 has passed.

Blended Learning replicates the WFH and WFA work environment. By having learning material available digitally, using Web 2.0 platforms for co-learning and sharing student created content with peers and the instructor, and coming together F2F for instruction and collaboration, this mode of learning is certainly in line with the WFH environment.

It is in providing within the higher education learning environment that which imitates the workplace that students are able to develop the graduate capabilities, skills and attributes that place them in the best position in the workforce. Blended Learning provides this learning environment.

Professor Andrew West, Dean, Universal Business School Sydney

---

[15] McCann, J (2020) Is A Blended Office Model The Future Of Work? *https://www.forbes.com/sites/forbesbusinesscouncil/2020/10/20/is-a-blended-office-model-the-future-of-work/?sh=1621091002ea*

[16] Johnson E (2021) Digital learning is real-world learning. That's why blended on-campus and online study is best, *https://theconversation.com/digital-learning-is-real-world-learning-thats-why-blended-on-campus-and-online-study-is-best-163002*

Chapter

3

The efficacy of online studies: Addressing the student dilemma

Ashok Chanda

INTRODUCTION

Online learning has become extremely *popular* recently owing to the current pandemic situation. Indeed, online is a *buzz word* among academics, educationists, students, and others who are associated with education in one form or another. Nonetheless, online education is not a new phenomenon. In 1960, at the University of Illinois, USA, online learning was first imparted using a network of computers interlinked[17], the Internet not being available at that time. The University of Phoenix, USA was a pioneer, offering bachelor and master qualifications online and many, thereafter, followed suit.

With technological advancement and high-speed internet, education has come right up to the doorstep – so to speak. Online learning has grown in leaps and bounds in the last decade, spreading like wildfire during the pandemic, and post pandemic, it will likely continue to grow. Almost all universities and institutions around the world have adopted online learning as a method of

[17] *https://adamasuniversity.ac.in/a-brief-history-of-online-education/*

delivery of their courses[18]. With students and teachers forced to remain away from classrooms, online learning has been the 'only way' to continue learning and teaching.

While the swift changes in mode of delivery transpired - shifting from classroom to online - universities and institutions worldwide adopted the online mode of delivery, and students have been left with no choice but to adapt to online learning, whether they like it or not. According to Harvard Professor, Daniel Schacter, as stated in a published proceeding of the National Academy of Sciences, 'online learning has exploded in popularity in the past few years,' and he writes, 'there remains shockingly little hard scientific data about how students learn in the virtual classroom.'[19]

EFFICACY OF ONLINE LEARNING

In fact, online learning is no more an option, but rather, a compulsion. Among student communities, not all students, in the first instance, like or want to remain online for all their studies. Typically, younger generation students miss their social environment, in-person interaction, in-class time, teacher-student engagements, and the feeling of being on a university campus.

With the race on of becoming successful online providers, by almost all universities and institutions across the world, a close look at the efficacy of online learning from the student point of view is worth exploring. Ultimately, the student dilemma must be addressed. Furthermore, it is appropriate to analyse if students who struggle will likely struggle further with the online mode.[20]

In 2004, well before the pandemic struck, a study where 76 graduates were surveyed to learn about student perception of useful and challenging characteristics of online learning, it was found that students were positive about course design, learner motivation, time management and 'comfortableness' associated

[18] Carey, K. (2020). Is everybody ready for the big migration to online college? Actually, no. The New York Times. *https://www.nytimes.com*
[19] *https://news.harvard.edu/gazette/story/2013/04/online-learning-its-different/*
[20] https://www.edweek.org/technology/opinion-how-effective-is-online-learning-what-the-research-does-and-doesnt-tell-us/2020/03

with online learning[21]. The same study also indicated that technical problems, a perceived lack of community and time constraints are some of the challenges associated with online learning. A large-scale literature study of 50 articles, just prior to the pandemic in 2019, examined each article and observed that 30 of them reported that the efficacy of online learning had been established, with well-planned, well-designed courses and programs for higher education institutes[22]. The most recent post pandemic study on real experience of students embarking on full online learning mode, revealed that there is a moderate to high level of acceptance of online learning among university students[23]. The latest study explored several key factors in online learning relating to learning motivation, learning readiness and student self-efficacy in participating in 'live' online learning during the coronavirus outbreak[24].

ADDRESSING THE STUDENT DILEMMA

The range of research before, during and after the pandemic provides a greater insight into why online learning is more effective from the student point of view. Some of the vital concluding reasons that emerge include -

Online learning means reduced stress. It does not demand waking up early or rushing through traffic to get to class on time. The programs are designed to be flexible which allows students to learn at their own pace. Students can rush past topics if they are comfortable and slow down with certain topics that require more

---

21 Liyang Song, Enrise S, Singleton, Jannette R, Hill, Myung Hwa Koh (2004) Improving Online Learning: Student perceptions of useful and Challenging characteristics, The Internet and Higher Education, 7(1): 59-70

22 Mayleen Dorcas B Castro and Gilbert M Tumibay (2021) A literature Review: Efficacy of online learning courses for higher education institution using meta-analysis, Education and Information technologies, 26, 1367-1385.

23 Sim, Sandra Phek-Lin; Sim, Hannah Phek-Khiok; Quah, Cheng-Sim (2020) Online Learning: A Post COVID-19 Alternative Pedagogy for University Students, Asian Journal of University Education, 16(4), 137-151

24 Yuk MingTang, Pen Chung Chen, Kris M.Y.Law, C.H.Wu, cYui-yipLau, Jieqi Guan, Dan He, G.T.S.Ho (2021) Comparative analysis of Student's live online learning readiness during the coronavirus (COVID-19) pandemic in the higher education sector, Computers & Education, 168, *https://doi.org/10.1016/j.compedu.2021.10421*

attention. This flexibility reduces stress which then permits students to focus on topics without having to worry about falling behind. As a result, students can build greater understanding of subjects.

Online learning provides a greater control of the study while it progresses. It provides a balance between work, family, and educational responsibilities. Online learning provides control when one listens to lectures, takes exams, and reviews course materials. It provides flexibility to study at any time and listen to lectures while commuting, for example. It also provides the opportunity to take a step back and review lectures from earlier in the course when students want to reinforce ideas and concepts.

Online learning means less time investment. Many students drop out from face-to-face courses due to time constraints. In addition, attending sessions by getting back and forth to classes, with attendance at a particular time, can be stressful. A Brandon Hall report on eLearning found that online learning typically requires 40-60% less time than learning in a formal classroom setting[25]. Online learning allows students to allocate the time they wish, depending on the way it best works for them.

Frequent assessments can reduce distractions. One of the great things about online learning is that assessments become more of an ongoing activity. This helps students immensely as regular short tests can encourage students to improve their engagement. Research from Harvard showed that using these short, regular tests halved student distraction and improved student overall retention of the content[26]. Moreover, with frequent assessments, lecturers are able to maintain close monitoring of the student progression.

Online learning offers a level playing field. In a perfect world, everyone would get the same level of lecturer attention. In the real world, there are always a handful of students who raise hands and draw the attention of the lecturer. With shy and/or reserved students, this does not occur, as they refrain from asking questions in classrooms. Nevertheless, online learning levels the field and gives every student an opportunity to ask their questions. This makes online learning a truly equal environment, where students do

---

25 *https://www.brandonhall.com/blogs/tag/e-learning/*

26 *https://news.harvard.edu/gazette/story/2013/04/online-learning-its-different/*

not have to worry about being the first to raise their hands in order to get the answers they need to master the material.

Students learn more than they do in traditional courses. IBM have found that participants learn five times more material in online learning courses using digital contents than in traditional face-to-face courses[27]. Since online courses give students full control over their own learning, students are able to work at their own speed. Generally, students work faster than they would do otherwise, and take in more information. They can move faster through areas of the course with which they feel comfortable, but slower through those areas where they need to dedicate a little more time.

Online learning increases retention rates. Many universities struggle to retain students throughout the full length of a course. The Research Institute of America has indicated that this is not the case with online learning[28]. Rather, online courses have increased student retention rates from anything ranging from 25% to 60%. Students being able to engage in online digital content with the associated flexibility to juggle their other commitments, has contributed to this growth in retention rates.

Online learning has become mainstream. Employers no longer differentiate between the value of an online degree versus that of a traditional bricks-and-mortar institution. For employers, the most important thing is the evident ability and skill a candidate brings to the job at hand. Furthermore, many organisations have relocated to remote locations. Depending on the profession, one may find employment with an organisation that could be halfway around the world. In such cases, demonstrated ability to perform effectively in an online environment is an additional asset brought to the table by candidates.

Online learning is more environmentally sustainable. Online learning is an effective option for students, but it is also the greener option. The Open University in Britain has uncovered that online courses equate to an average of 90% less energy and 85% fewer

---

[27] *https://www.ibm.com/blogs/think/2020/03/pandemic-impacts-millions-of-students-how-digital-learning-can-help/*

[28] *https://www.forbes.com/sites/paycom/2017/02/14/learning-management-systems-101-rethinking-your-approach-to-employee-training/?sh=d63db37755bc*

CO_2 emissions per student than traditional in-person courses[29]. This certainly makes online learning a more environmentally friendly contribution with regard to the global footprint of climate change. Promoting and engaging in online learning can help both individuals and institutions to contribute effectively to sustainability.

ONLINE LEARNING – HERE TO STAY

An estimated 290 million students have been impacted globally as a consequence of the COVID-19 pandemic which, in turn, has created an unprecedented impact with regard to the speed of disruption in education. On a global scale, in almost all countries, schools and universities have chosen to leave behind face-to-face teaching and to transform in favour of online learning.

The closing of classroom doors came with a shock at a time when students were preparing for their upcoming tests. It has provided an opportunity to expand access to online learning with technology and digitised content for both lecturers and students.

With rapidly changing technology and the speed at which businesses must operate to be competitive in a global digital economy, it is clear that online learning for students is essential in order to remain competitive in the workplace. It is accepted that online learning is not the only way to learn, but that online programs provide increased access, and so, the cost of continued learning to a wider population of students is reduced. Online learning is here to stay.

Associate Professor Ashok Chanda, Provost, UBSS Online Campus, Group Colleges Australia

[29] *https://www3.open.ac.uk/events/3/2005331_47403_o1.pdf*

Section 2:

The Response Papers

The renaissance of 'the Virtual Conservatorium'

Ian Bofinger

INTRODUCTION

In 2002, almost two decades ago, Emeritus Professor Greg Whateley and I embarked on a project that we initially named *i*Con, where units at the *Central Queensland Conservatorium of Music* were delivered in a variety of modes to suit student learning requirements, the key elements of *i*Con being *i*nternet, *i*ntensive, *i*ndustry and *i*nnovation[30]. This concept then further developed to become Australia's first Virtual Conservatorium, which began operating under the tagline of 'Anywhere, Anyhow, Anytime' in 2004.

The uses of the *i*nternet in the *i*Con project were threefold, as an asynchronous (non-time dependent), synchronous (real-time) delivery medium, with the inclusion of online software training packages. The *i*ntensive mode considered the re-allocation of the equivalent hours of existing weekly, face-to-face (F2F) class lectures into an intense, saturated delivery. This also enabled access to *i*ndustry-based professional practitioners. All this required an *i*nnovative approach to what traditionally was a conservative Performing Arts education environment. As expected, this concept

[30] *https://acquire.cqu.edu.au/articles/report/Projects_iCon_and_Uptech_Creating_infrastructure_for_the_virtual_Conservatorium/13429160*

was met by a polarised response from many conservatorium academics of the day.

But as the novelist Stephen King (2005)[31] wrote, "sooner or later, everything old is new again". The impact of the COVID-19 pandemic on higher education in the performing arts has meant that all institutions have had to adapt to new lecture delivery paradigms. Whilst authors such as Li (2021)[32] outline their latest, cutting-edge modes of delivery at the Hong Kong Academy of Performing Arts as "Blended, m-Learning and Hybrid Learning", it is notable that these rely on the same key elements of the original Virtual Conservatorium initiative which came some 20 years before.

In my current position as Executive Dean and CEO of the Australian Academy of Music and Performing Arts (AMPA), I am ultimately responsible for the ongoing delivery of the undergraduate and postgraduate degrees in both Dance and Music. This paper is presented as a case study of the current delivery methods that are being utilized to maintain and evolve the undergraduate Bachelor of Music degree during the volatile times that we have experienced/are experiencing in 2020 and 2021.

As a brief overview of the degree, the overall structure can be broken down into units that either have a strong **practical and performance** focus: (Principal and Second Study, Performance Class, Ensemble and Performance Art) and those that are predominantly **academic** in structure: (Harmony & Analysis, Music History and Ear Training).

PERFORMANCE UNITS

Principal and second study

These units are traditionally delivered in a one-to-one studio environment. The mentor-based relationship that evolves from students working individually with a professional practitioner from the music industry is the cornerstone of AMPA's tertiary music education.

---

31 *https://www.smartbrief.com/original/2018/08/whats-old-new-again*
32 *https://link.springer.com/article/10.1007/s10639-021-10612-1*

During the COVID lockdown periods, synchronous video-conferencing applications have enabled the training to continue, with the choice of application at the discretion of the staff and student involved, and this has predominantly been delivered via *Zoom*, but also via *Microsoft Teams*, *Skype,* and *FaceTime.*

Ensemble

The key goals of this series of units involve the development of collaboration and musical communication when performing in a group environment. This may be a contemporary band, a classical piano trio, or a music theatre company. In a typical mode of delivery, this is taught face-to-face in small groups with a lecturer directing the class.

Moving this to online raised significant issues that had to be addressed. If attempting to use traditional video-conferencing technologies, the lag time of each individual connection differs so dramatically that it renders the process ineffective. Blackburn and Hewitt (2020)[33] report that the use of network music performance (NMP) systems is still "marred by the issue of latency, which remains the primary hindrance for the perceived success of these types of collaborations".

Whilst the AMPA staff have access to Internet speeds of approximately 400Mbps whilst on campus, most students are operating on domestic NBN or 4G at speeds of 20Mbps or less. AMPA tested low latency software applications, but even with the automatic buffering designed to align the performance, the audio and video compression algorithms were significant enough to detract from the prescribed outcomes of the unit.

To overcome these problems, it was decided to focus on developing the specific collaborative skills required for a professional studio session musician, these being the ability to either *Multitrack* - i.e., layering of parts, particularly suitable for contemporary ensembles - or *Music Minus One* - using a guide backing track. These are created by conversion of digital media files that have the student's individual part removed from the audio.

---

33 *https://onlineinnovationsjournal.com/streams/visual-and-performing-arts/63209b3a0ef5fedf.html*

The student then records only their part whilst hearing the rest of the ensemble via headphones. A composite file of the individual acoustic recordings can be created by layering each of the individual parts once they have been uploaded into the LMS (Learning Management System).

Performance class

The didactic intent of this set of units is to experience the process of a concert environment. In a typical trimester, this is achieved by utilizing AMPA's professional theatre stage which includes incandescent and intelligent lighting, digital audio, and industry-current staff.

The symbiotic outcome of this unit also enables the students who are not performing on stage on a particular week to complete a critical review and reflection of the concert items. The rubrics used are identical to those that are used by the panel of examiners for the end of unit performance exams for Principal Study, so the process enables the students to experience the marking process firsthand from the assessor's point of view.

During the lockdown periods, the students have not been able to access the theatre, and so, have had to record their performances from home, upload their MP4 and submit a URL link. AMPA then combines these individual performances into a 'concert' video and distributes this via the LMS, eCon for the class to complete the secondary reflective task.

Although this is not ideal, the students and staff, as identified by Whateley (2020)[34] as either 'digital natives, immigrants or convicts,' have still managed to meet all of the unit's outcomes and obligations.

Performance art

These units are created for students to cultivate a synthesis of stylistically appropriate musical performance. This is achieved by dissecting and analysing genre-significant works and then applying

[34] *https://www.campusreview.com.au/2020/09/full-marks-for-educators-the-digital-convicts-of-covid-19/*

these concepts when performing these pieces in a staged performance. Students then align their practical development of technical skills with the academic understanding of the stylistic components of the genre.

To deliver this unit during the current pandemic limitations, a tripartite blended learning mode has been implemented. Online lectures have been created and uploaded, music minus one MP3s have also been developed so students can rehearse their specific part along with a unique backing track, and the final assessment comes after the culmination of an intensive delivery period in the last week of the course.

Rather than opt for ongoing videoconference sessions to prepare for the final performance, the F2F interactions gained by the intensive classes have been considered to be educationally stronger and also allow for a true sense of occasion. AMPA also considers that maintaining the student's academic progress and mental health and wellbeing are equally important during the period. As David and Phillips (2021)[35] note, "A lack of equity around digital connection resulted in some students not being able to access their learning. Other environmental factors in the home prevented some students from engaging with their work in a meaningful way." By combining these three delivery modes, students can work through the materials at their own pace, and the intensive component encapsulates the learning with a concert performance of the 12 works studied during the trimester.

ACADEMIC UNITS

Harmony & analysis

In 2020, these units which concentrate on musicianship (reading, writing and analysis of music), were delivered as a Hybrid lecture. In this mode, the lecturer delivered the class simultaneously to an on-campus F2F audience and online (via Zoom). This delivery mode still allows for synchronous communication between lecturer and students. AMPA further enhanced this to be an 'extended

[35] *https://www.campusreview.com.au/2021/07/new-research-looks-at-how-performing-arts-teachers-and-students-are-coping-in-a-time-of-remote-learning/*

hybrid mode', where lecture recordings are also to be used as an asynchronous study resource.

Software applications had to be deployed to further enable the digital upload of music notation. As many of the commercial packages are either platform specific or financially burdensome for the students, it was decided to use the multi-platform, open-source application, *Musescore*[36].

Music history

AMPA delivers over 12 different Music History units. These were traditionally delivered as a F2F lecture. The density and volume of the material that was required to be delivered meant that the lecture was predominantly a dissemination of the information using PowerPoint presentations as the stimulus material for the lecture. This left little or no time for questions, let alone significant discussion or debate.

During 2020, AMPA moved into a blended mode of delivery for these units. The existing PowerPoint files were extensively developed to become similar to a documentary with audio-visual annotations, enriched multimedia (external edited/short video sections) and a conversion to MP4 for viewing on computer, television, or mobile phone. The material can be observed at the student's preferred time and repeat viewings are possible. The 'lecture' is then followed up with a short Zoom based tutorial.

Our experience found that although this involved extra time (and finances) to cover the initial creation of the material, over an extended period, these resources can be easily finessed and updated for future dissemination of the academic content. This has meant that the tutorial has become the essential tool for synthesis of information. Owston et al. (2019)[37] recommend that a successful Blended Learning delivery comprises of 80% high quality online learning integrated with 20% classroom teaching. The paradigm shift to the focus being on synthesis via the tutorial interaction has seen a stronger sense of engagement by the student body.

---

36 *https://musescore.org/en/download*

37 *https://link.springer.com/article/10.1007/s10758-020-09477-z*

Ear training

It took the COVID-19 pandemic for staff to evolve from their long-established pedagogical comfort zone to consider delivering this unit using blended technologies. Ear Training units develop aural recognition skills for both music notation and sight-reading. These have been delivered for centuries by Conservatoire via a F2F mode, with the lecturer presenting from a grand piano. As the Conservatoire name implies, the model has been deliberately restrictive in development to 'conserve' the old traditions. AMPA has not replaced this proven mode of aural training, but instead, enhanced and modernised the delivery. Studying via a blended mode of software-based learning in addition to tutorial-based learning, students now have access to the self-paced teaching modules incorporated into the software *Auralia*[38], alongside attending the traditional tutorial-based class. (The grand piano, however, has been replaced by an electronic keyboard that can seamlessly deliver both acoustic performance and digital recordings for online transmissions.)

In this instance, AMPA is blurring the lines between 'Hybrid' and 'Blended' modes, where students also have the option of attending the tutorial 'in person' or via *Zoom*. The tutorials are also recorded and uploaded into the LMS for student viewing at their discretion.

The 2021 Renaissance of the notion of *The Virtual Conservatorium* (*Anywhere, Anyhow, Anytime*) has demonstrated that the concept was indeed ahead of its time. The significant development in computational power and digital transmission speeds over the past 20 years has enabled the original notions of *i*Con to become mainstream in today's Higher Education sector. The four pillars upon which it was founded, ***i*nternet**, ***i*ntensive**, ***i*ndustry** and ***i*nnovation**, are the foundations upon which current tertiary courses are now being constructed.

Professor Ian Bofinger, Executive Dean and CEO of AMPA, the Australian Academy of Music and Performing Arts

38 *https://www.risingsoftware.com/auralia*

Online learning and the organisation: key challenges defined

Anurag Kanwar

INTRODUCTION

Online learning has become increasingly popular and/or common as higher education providers move to teach successfully in a pandemic. There are numerous articles in relation to the challenges and/or barriers to learning on the part of students[39]. There is one important stakeholder whose voice is absent in all this commentary - that is, the organisation (the higher education provider) itself. This paper will look at the challenges of online learning with respect to academic staff and what is required from the organisation in terms of support and resources.

ONLINE LEARNING AND COVID-19

The rapid adoption of online learning by Australia's higher education sector was an enormous undertaking at a time when staff and students were facing a range of pressures stemming from the

39 GILLETT-SWAN, Jenna. The Challenges of Online Learning: Supporting and Engaging the Isolated Learner. Journal of Learning Design, [S.l.], v. 10, n. 1, p. 20-30, jan. 2017. ISSN 1832-8342. Available at: *https://www.jld.edu.au/article/view/293/269*

pandemic's impact on everyday life. That COVID-19 disrupted the provision of higher education is a given. Time will tell how history judges this disruption, but prior to 2020, the use of educational videos, though increasing, was often cursory and was generally seen as an add-on to traditional methods, rather than the main event in teaching.

It is clear from the most recent Quality Indicators for Learning and Teaching (QILT) results that independent providers[40] rose to the challenges of online learning better than established universities[41]. This could be because independent providers tend to be smaller than universities and therefore able to adapt more quickly. Nonetheless, there were many challenges that arose for all educational providers across the sector. These will now be considered.

ORGANISATIONAL CHALLENGES

IT

The organisation will need to ensure that it has a strong internet connection which is secure. In addition, what systems are in place if the internet fails to work and how will the teaching be managed? What risk mitigation (if any) strategies have been implemented?

The organisation will also need to provide access to a full range of support services, including (but not limited to) -

- email support
- live chat
- technical support on the ground.

This requires substantial investment on the part of the organisation. In addition, a number of organisations do not have 'in house' IT support, and so, this needs actioning as soon as possible. If the organisation has outsourced its IT support, are the staff members familiar with what to do in the event of an outage?

---

40 Those higher education institutions who are not self-accrediting

41 *https://ihea.edu.au/news/independent-higher-education-providers-best-in-country-qilt-results/* accessed 27 July 2021

Teaching from home

The pandemic has shifted people to working from home[42] - a necessity especially where there are lockdowns. These lockdowns raise particular nuisances which need to be considered[43] -

- the employer (or organisation) needs to provide guidance on a safe working environment
- the employer (or organisation) needs to maintain communication
- the employer needs to provide resources to manage mental health and other concerns

A recent court case found an employer was responsible for an employee's death at the hands of the employee's partner. The employer had a duty of care towards all employees, including protecting them from family violence[44].

Teaching is not traditionally considered an online activity. As a result, the quality in the teaching can vary. For example, one teaching organisation relied on the individual academics using their own electronic resources[45], not providing much in the way of IT support, the argument being that most people have their own electronic resources in any event. The response from the students was mixed. Student feedback indicated that they were extremely dissatisfied with their experience, noting that some lecturers used their phones to speak to the slides[46]. What was absent was any student engagement and any interaction with the class.

One organisation simply shipped laptops and other audio equipment to academics' houses via Uber. This ensured that the academic was teaching from a secure device and was compatible with the Learning Management System. A draw back to this approach was that staff were not given instructions on how to assemble or connect the devices. Another drawback was some of

---

42 *https://blog.hubspot.com/marketing/productivity-tips-working-from-home* accessed 29 July 2021

43 *https://www.nsw.gov.au/covid-19/safe-workplaces/workers/working-from-home* accessed 29 July 2021

44 *https://www.hrmonline.com.au/employment-law/family-domestic-violence-working-from-home/* accessed 29 July 2021

45 *https://www.ubss.edu.au/articles/2021/may/online-teaching-a-tale-of-two-institutions/*

46 *https://www.ubss.edu.au/articles/2021/may/online-teaching-a-tale-of-two-institutions/*

the equipment was returned to the organisation damaged or locked as it had been used for personal purposes rather than the specific task of teaching.

Yet, another teaching organisation simply insisted that the academics come on to campus. Academics were provided with the requisite paperwork (as essential workers). This ensured that the employee had access to a safe working environment, coupled with IT support and infrastructure. The organisation in question has a well-equipped and maintained studio environment with tracking cameras as well as interactive whiteboards[47]. For the students, this environment most mimicked the classroom experience. In terms of risk, the third approach is perhaps the least risky, as academics are in their familiar learning environment.

Human resources

From a human resources perspective, the organisation will need to consider the individual employment contracts of the academics. For example, does the contract stipulate the mode of delivery?

If the contract explicitly states that teaching will be face to face, to change that delivery mode may be viewed as a breach of contract. In addition, the organisation will need to consider the needs of 'independent contractors' if any are used. What were the terms of engagement? As a matter of best practice, any changes to the contract need to be communicated to all parties and consent must be obtained for any changes.

Another risk for the organisation is what occurs when an employee refuses to sign any amendment to a contract? This will mean that their employment has been terminated. So, it is prudent for an organisation to have a backup plan in the event of this occurrence. This may mean having a list of academics who can teach online at short notice.

Training for staff on using equipment

To successfully teach online requires a certain level of technological proficiency. This includes the ability to understand online

[47] *https://www.ubss.edu.au/media/2670/understanding-hybrid-delivery.pdf*

communication etiquette, as well as the log in process, and delivering the lectures in a style that is communicative and informed. Staff may need to be trained in such matters *prior* to the commencement of online delivery.

Lecturers will need to be trained in delivery of 'live presentations'. Repetition, coughing and head down are not acceptable[48]. The lectures need to be prepared in advance and presented well. Teaching material 'on the run' is undesirable from the perspective of a quality learning experience.

Regulatory environment

The organisation also needs to consider the regulatory environment. For example, does the regulatory body, such as, TEQSA, need to be notified of the move to online learning? And, if so, when should the regulatory body be informed? If an organisation notifies the regulator, does the organisation need to wait 'for approval' for online delivery?

Noting that in a pandemic it is actually a physical impossibility to teach face to face, what are the liabilities for the organisation (and/or directors) if it fails to disclose? These matters need to be considered in greater detail by the organisation in the move to online delivery.

Online learning is here to stay[49]. The pandemic has shifted the traditional modes of delivery for education. Organisations that adapt quickly will be the ones that will thrive. From an organisational perspective, there are some key challenges that remain and need to be addressed.

Anurag Kanwar, Director of Compliance and Continuous Improvement, Group Colleges Australia

[48] *https://www.ubss.edu.au/media/2670/understanding-hybrid-delivery.pdf*
[49] *https://www.ubss.edu.au/media/2695/the-efficacy-of-online-studies.pdf*

Alternative delivery modes for international students

Greg Whateley

INTRODUCTION

As a consequence of the COVID-19 pandemic, there has been an involuntary shift to online learning. In turn, this has also highlighted and facilitated a range of other alternative mode delivery mechanisms for international students, sometimes referred to as flexible modes of delivery and other times alternative modes of delivery. The traditional face to face mode has been overtaken (certainly for a period of time) with a range of alternative arrangements that cater for lockdowns and community restrictions.

Prior to the pandemic, international education (onshore in Australia) was in face-to-face mode, with strict regulations around the percentage of classes international students were allowed to complete online, and so, regulations surrounding attendance at face-to-face classes, the extent of employment hours permitted on a student visa, and the requirement of 50% progression rates in order to maintain the student visa, were integral to meeting these regulations. Much of this was dictated by the ESOS Act 2000 and the supporting National Code[50]. Then, of course, everything changed! In truth, there has been a slow and determined movement

[50] *https://internationaleducation.gov.au/regulatory-information/Education-Services-for-Overseas-Students-ESOS-Legislative-Framework/National-Code/Pages/default.aspx*

in the regulations over a period of time. Matters such as attendance have been downplayed for a number of years, for example.

The so-called alternative (flexible) modes of delivery - Blended Learning (bLearning)[51], Online Learning (eLearning)[52] and Hybrid Learning (hLearning)[53] - were viewed as domestic products with little if any application for international students studying in Australia. This too is no longer the case! The rapid shift to online learning that occurred created a new precedent that is likely to stay with us for some time. The prediction is that even on a return to face-to-face learning in the years ahead, the percentage of study permitted online for international students will grow to 50% of the load. This represents a significant shift in thinking.

Tertiary institutions were required to move rapidly into eLearning - as a matter of survival. Some of the better prepared organisations (and many had been dabbling in alternative/flexible options for some time) managed to deviate even further and utilise the other two modes with varying degrees of success. Sector reports suggest the more flexibly inclined have fared best in the so-called international student crisis. There are a number of reasons for this. As the Australian Government regulations loosened on the number of paid hours that international students can work in country - from 40 hours per fortnight to unlimited - the demand, of course, for flexibility has grown significantly.

THE PERILS OF ENFORCED ELEARNING

The sudden switch to online (eLearning) caused a considerable level of distress for many institutions and, in particular, academic staff. For many, this was the 'end of the world' as they knew it. Understandably, for staff who had been teaching international students for many years in the traditional face to face mode, this was indeed a precarious and uninvited demand. For others it was the opportunity to put in place a variety of modes that could still maintain high levels of student engagement. Learner engagement

[51] *https://www.ubss.edu.au/media/2716/what-is-meant-by-blended-learning.pdf*
[52] *https://www.ubss.edu.au/media/2695/the-efficacy-of-online-studies.pdf*
[53] *https://www.ubss.edu.au/media/2670/understanding-hybrid-delivery.pdf*

(coupled with the student experience) - remember - is perceived as the end game.

My own institution appears to have fared well with the most recent (July 2021) Student Feedback on Units scoring 4.41/5 (the highest score since records were kept, that is, from T1, 2016), and Staff Satisfaction scoring 4.3/5, and 92% of students noting that they would prefer to stay online for the duration. Sector feedback suggests the aggregate is lower than this.

THE PITFALLS ASSOCIATED WITH RETURNING TO FACE-TO-FACE CLASSES ON CAMPUS

The return to campus movement has taken quite a few hits with flash lockdowns across the country. Some of the enforced lockdowns (Victoria has had five to date) have varied in length from 10 days to four months, the key issue being the unpredictability of closures (and durations), especially in some states with hair-trigger border closures accompanied by circuit breaker lockdowns - both with very short fuses - and very little time to prepare. In this context, face to face options seem dim.

A number of providers have recently formally announced they will continue online learning for the rest of 2021 - the news has not been well received in many quarters. What the decision has done though, is provide a degree of certainty and consistency - not a bad development in itself. It would appear online learning (and the associated variations) are here to stay for some time. Some predict that this will endure well into 2021, and even into 2022.

THE FUTURE OF HLEARNING

Hybrid Learning (hLearning) appears to be the future - or certainly the mode for the next couple of years. The model is based on delivering live sessions online with the option for students to attend face to face by choice, not unlike the concept of 'live to air' television.

The enormous advantage of the mode is the quick (and relatively easy) response mechanism to future lockdowns and restrictions. The acceptance of the notion of high-end hygiene and COVID safety are also well accommodated in this mode. The worst-case scenario is that the option of sitting in a classroom during a live delivery is suspended for a given period - but teaching and learning continues online without interruption.

The mode also provides students with the all-important option of on campus/off campus delivery. This is well received by students. For staff it requires delivery on site throughout the trimester/semester. This is less well received by staff, but for many, regarded as a necessary evil. The issue of staff teaching on site is all about ensuring a quality output, complete with the necessary technology standard and IT support.

STAFF AND STUDENT PERCEPTIONS

At the heart of the COVID-19 scenario is the impact that the changes have had on student experience. There is a mixed response to online learning. At the same time, there has also been considerable acceptance of the mode, not only in Australia, but internationally[54]. This has been accompanied by an acknowledgement of the validity and currency of online learning (along with variations).

There has been a considerable focus on student and staff response to online learning and teaching - and the outcomes vary from institution to institution. Mechanisms, such as, student feedback on units surveys; staff satisfaction surveys; satisfaction with online learning surveys; national QILT surveys relating to the overall student experience (the 2021 data collection commences in July 2021 and is to be published in early 2022); industry group surveys; and a plethora of research surveys (both private and public) are all useful tools for gathering intelligence on and around student/staff satisfaction.

The best approach is internal survey. It is essential that all providers have a clear understanding of their own student/staff needs and respond quickly and appropriately to the needs

[54] *http://thirdway.imgix.net/pdfs/one-year-later-covid-19s-impact-on-current-and-future-college-students.pdf*

expressed. If supported appropriately, the outcomes and levels of satisfaction can be highly credible and rewarding for all stakeholders.

Emeritus Professor Greg Whateley, Deputy Vice Chancellor, Group Colleges Australia

The art of digitalising online content: Making learning content effective

Ashok Chanda

INTRODUCTION

It is always exciting to see how some social media content becomes viral and, in turn, what becomes popular and what becomes a 'favourite'. There could be a number of reasons associated with its popularity index, however, one can observe that the popular/favourite content is in some way different from the rest, and therefore, gains tremendous attention of people at large.

A scholarly research work published by Berger and Milkman (2012) on what makes online content go viral used a data set of all the *New York Times* articles published over a three-month period. The authors then examined how the emotion of the readers shapes virality[55]. The results indicate that positive content is more viral than negative content - though, the relationship between emotion and social transmission is complex. In today's world, a news channel just dreaming of deploying a camera and simply filming a newsreader on the evening news is not a sensible proposition. Without narration, without using multiple camera angles, cutaway

[55] Berger J. and Milkman K. L. (2012) What makes online content Viral? Journal of Marketing Research, Vol. XLIX, 192 –205. *https://doi.org/10.1509/jmr.10.0353*

views and close-ups of the presenter, viewers would lose interest almost instantly. The game has changed.

In the online learning space, the same issue applies to the learning content. If the learning content is built around positivity and taking into account the student emotional perspective, it is likely to gain more positive attention by students. Content, then, must be interesting or practically useful, both of which are positively linked to virality. How prominently content is featured, determines how it can build student interest and attention.

This article focuses on what constitutes effective online learning experiences. It reflects on elements in design of course content, learning tasks, and pedagogical approaches, which all contribute to a positive online learning experience.

ART OF DIGITALISING ONLINE CONTENT

There is a sharp misconception among online course providers as to what is 'Digitisation of content' and 'Digitalisation of content'. 'Digitisation of content' describes the process of basically switching tangible content into a digital format, while 'Digitalisation of content' describes an intrinsic adaptation of the learning resources best suiting the learning needs of the online students which is effective and experiential[56]. Digitalising content involves structural changes in the content, correctly adapted to a new format with its own set of norms.

Digitalisation is way beyond just transposing a course into digital content. It requires a rethink on how the course material is delivered. The content must be designed to create a dynamic, interactive learning platform with content that will engage students. Proper structuring of the course is essential for achieving these goals. The learning content should be accessible to students at any time from any place and on any compatible electronic device using internet. Students should be able to download the content for an offline study option.

---

[56] *https://www.forbes.com/sites/jasonbloomberg/2018/04/29/digitization-digitalization-and-digital-transformation-confuse-them-at-your-peril/?sh=fb2466a2f2c7*

Online learning generally provides two options - asynchronous (not existing or occurring at the same time) and synchronous (existing or occurring at the same time). Both options are designed around two types of learning contents - eLearning content and webinars[57].

Unlike face-to-face teaching, online learning does not have lecturers and students physically present in the classroom. Students virtually access content and lecturers virtually deliver. The face-to-face delivery has two prominent ingredients, one being the presence of lecturers who share the learning experience, with students having freedom to interact with lecturers resolving learning queries. The second ingredient is learning texts (including prescribed textbooks and related presentations and case studies). These resources are predominantly used during delivery in the face-to-face classroom. In the online learning delivery environment, both of these formats are missing. Lecturers do appear during live webinars, but the interaction with students generally does not occur.

CONTENT IS KING IN ONLINE LEARNING

In the virtual learning environment 'content is the king'. What content is made available and how the content is presented will play a vital role, as online resources are the two most important factors contributing to effective student learning[58]. All content should be made available for students to access both online and offline, providing students with the option of how they wish to learn.

Most courses vary greatly in terms of length, weekly workload, and the number of course modules provided. On average, a subject within a university undergraduate or postgraduate course has a duration of thirteen (13) to fifteen (15) weeks. Each week consists of 1 to 2 hours of coursework. During the weekly planned study load, both asynchronous and synchronous learning is weaved together. For example, each week webinars are delivered by the lecturer - synchronous learning is provided - covering one or two

[57] *https://online.osu.edu/resources/learn/whats-difference-between-asynchronous-and-synchronous-learning*

[58] *https://www.udemy.com/course/how-to-write-the-best-online-content/*

topics of the subjects, and lecturers explain the topics in webinar format. At the same time, in the asynchronous format, learning content of the same one or two topics is placed on the learning management system to which students are given access.

On average, digitalised content of a subject consists of activities, such as, a course outline, assessment guide and topics summary. The learning contents for each topic is developed with a topic presentation, summary readings explaining topics, case studies, real-life examples, short videos, research articles, self-practice tests, quizzes with multiple choice answers and a range of supplementary reading. Each of these is designed with an appropriate presentation form, such as, using multi-colour graphic design, fonts, graphs, tables, pictures, photos, icons, caricatures, and symbols, in order to keep consistency with content and ensure student interest is maintained. Using 'voice over' of lecturers, video of lecturers in a classroom setting and infographic presentations, designed specially related to topics, adds interest for learners. Along with the above, recordings of regular webinars delivered as synchronous study, also placed in the learning content, can be accessed alongside digitized contents by students at all times.

Assessment design in online learning must be developed keeping in mind the nature of online learning, as opposed to the physical paper-pencil and invigilated test environment. Computer based online tests are ideal for assessments, however, short quizzes, summative assessment assignments (all with a submission time frame) are also most appropriate methods for inclusion.

The digitalised content must be built-in, keeping course specifications and requirements in mind at all times. It is certainly possible to create more content as extra support for learners, but the risk of losing student engagement increases proportionally. Content is fighting for student attention alongside the course requirements and assessments. In online studies, students are constantly tempted to move away from the content and open a new browser tab and check out what is happening on Facebook or YouTube. Keeping course content short and succinct is the best deterrent to straying in the digitalisation strategy.

INTRICACIES OF ONLINE LEARNING CONTENT

Use of instructional design concept

There are many reasons why the instructional design concept requires that learning is more safe, certain, thorough, and expeditious than otherwise[59], at the same time, facilitating the learning process, as learners will require less time, incur less risk, and invest less energy than those who learned from the world without assistance.

Optimising Learning Management System

In a recent study conducted by Fearnley et al., (2020) investigating factors that influenced adoption of a learning management system by higher education providers using the technology acceptance model, incorporates three external constructs - system quality; perceived self-efficacy; and facilitating conditions[60]. There are many elements that go into a successful building of digitalisation of content. The Learning Management System is a content hub, but it must combine with academic support and student support mechanisms to give content the best chance of reaching the right people at the right time[61]. It should be noted that content represents an online course as a product that the students consume. Putting every piece of content that is digitalised at the heart of every piece of content created becomes essential.

Choose the Right Educational Technology

Learning with the right kind of education technology enhances students' learning abilities. There are three types of interaction between learner, instructor, and computer[62]. The interaction

---

59 *https://www.tandfonline.com/doi/citedby/10.1080/13562517.2021.1872527?scroll=top&needAccess=true*

60 Fearnley, Marissa R.; Amora, Johnny T. (2020), Learning Management System Adoption in Higher Education Using the Extended Technology Acceptance Model, IAFOR Journal of Education, 8(2), 89-106.

61 *https://link.springer.com/content/pdf/10.1007/s10758-020-09475-1.pdf*

62 *https://eric.ed.gov/?id=EJ1277763*

between learner and computer can be enhanced by using flashcards, RSS, YouTube videos, Add Blocks and FAQs. Interaction between learner and instructor can be enhanced with lessons, quizzes, projects, conference with video chat and quick email. Interaction between learner and learner can be enhanced by using chats, forums, blogs, and glossaries.

Revision Procedures

Once the content is digitalised and ready to offer online, it is important to run various revision procedures to ensure that the content digitalised is meeting quality requirements. This would include, for example, conducting a survey evaluating each eLearning module for course and site design, navigation, and design aesthetics. Post survey, a panel of experts should review the digitalised course. This process should include subject matter experts, instructional designers, eLearning developers, etc. Based on their constructive feedback, appropriate revision of the digitalised course needs to be carried out before making it available to students. Most importantly, digitalised coursework must be further revised using student constructive feedback.

Protecting online content

It is important to protect digitalised courseware from infringements. It is advisable to use Safeguard Secure PDF Writer and choose the various protection options, such as stop printing, allow printing, or limit the number of prints, adding dynamic watermarks to viewed and/or printed pages. To further protect online content, organizations could build expiring e-learning courses, where a specific date, number of views, number of prints, or number of days after accessing the content determine the length of time it remains available to the student.

FUTURE TRENDS IN DIGITALISATION

With the ongoing advancement of technology, there are new trends emerging in online learning content digitalisation all the time. The newest trends around developing games-based learning, gamification of learning content[63], simulation learning[64], and using artificial intelligence (AI) and virtual reality[65] are gaining momentum and, in turn, re-shaping digitalisation of learning content.

There are endless debates about the needs of the new generation learner and the methods and instruments that online education providers should offer in order to satisfy these needs and interests. Every year, lecturers and developers face new terms, ideas, and concepts that emerge as if they were the only definitive solution to all the problems in online education and learning. The truth is digitalisation is not the only solution to all the problems that exist and to resolving online education matters. There is no single or unique solution that will improve the teaching-learning process entirely.

Associate Professor Ashok Chanda, Provost, UBSS Online Campus, Group Colleges Australia

[63] *https://www.teacheracademy.eu/blog/game-based-learning/*

[64] *https://www.ncbi.nlm.nih.gov/pmc/articles/PMC2966567/*

[65] Jee Hyun Lee, Eunkyoung Yang, Zhong Yuan Sun. (2021) Using an Immersive Virtual Reality Design Tool to Support Cognitive Action and Creativity: Educational Insights from Fashion Designers. The Design Journal 24:4, pages 503-524.

Chapter

8

Future Experience: Why we will no longer 'go to university'

Jim Mienczakowski

INTRODUCTION

If not now, then soon. If not for all, then for most. If not in its entirety, then in its majority. Higher Education will be increasingly delivered and experienced both asynchronously and synchronously via innovative technologies, and physical attendance at any geographically located campus will no longer be the norm. *'Going to university'* will ultimately mean something different to what we currently understand and experience a university education to be.

This paper discusses some of the social, economic, and cultural drivers of technological change in higher education provision. It foreshadows a growing role for smaller, private providers who are research aware (but not, necessarily, research focussed) in meeting the increasing needs of a global majority of students seeking accredited, and workplace engaged, qualifications. Herein, e, b and hLearning, as discussed in other chapters, will become essential as key entry level competencies for those seeking to work and study in the higher education world of the next decade or so.

FUTURIST NOTIONS

Undoubtedly, futurists, such as, Alvin Toffler and the writer and philosopher, Aldous Huxley[66], have long envisaged scientific developments which would significantly change society. Even futuristic television series may have influenced the direction and nature of subsequent technological development. For example, Gene Roddenberry's 'Star Trek' - first arriving on our TV screens back in 1966 - introduced us to (amongst numerous other concepts) the 'Communicator': the small handheld device which we now call the *mobile phone*. Futurists, since the 1930s, have been predicting mechanisation (technology) replacing human beings on industrial production lines and in menial labouring roles. Such futuristic predictions have repeatedly come true.

Futurist notions about potential changes to schooling, education and learning are equally impacted by scientific and technological advancements, as well as by the biggest driver of them all - the economy. But multiple drivers for change need to be engaged in order for transformation and development to become *probable*, and the necessary change-drivers seem to now be in place for eL, bL and hL to become the dominant delivery methods for achieving and delivering tertiary qualifications.

A HISTORY OF ECONOMIC CHANGE DRIVERS

Mass public education systems providing state-funded education to everyone did not generally eventuate in the western world until the late 1800s (Ramierez, F.O. & Boli, J.,1987)[67]. Typically, however, the education provided by state public schools in the western world was only concerned with the *basic skilling of an industrial workforce* and fell far below the standards required to enter university.

---

[66] Aldous Huxley wrote Brave New World in 1932. It foreshadowed a number of social and scientific developments (including invitro fertilisation, genetic cloning, helicopters and genetically modified babies, as well as antidepressants and fascism) before they became realities.

[67] F.O. Ramirez & J. Boli, (1987). The political construction of mass schooling: European origins and worldwide institutionalization. F.O. Ramirez & J. Boli (1987). Sociology of education, 1987– JSTOR *https://www.jstor.org/stable/2112615*

It wasn't until the 1980s that Australia's government intentionally doubled the numbers of school students completing Year 12 to boost the totals eligible for tertiary studies (C. King, 2021)[68]. The economy was the change-driver - it needed more graduates in order to grow.

Currently, as COVID-19 drags on, many graduates (in the western world) are complaining[69] that their tertiary studies and investments in HECS debts have not been worthwhile[70]. Some qualifications being offered in the public system don't meet students' increasing demands for quality teaching and employability[71] - though, it can be equally argued that the impacts of COVID-19 haven't helped in this. Again, the gap between graduate expectations and employment is another economic driver for further change.

MAJOR FACTORS

The French philosopher, Louis Althusser[72] (1970-2014), observed that in times of economic duress, it is often the case that a government's first response is to cut costs and reduce funding to public education. Across Australia, universities have certainly experienced reduced government funding since the 1980s, but they have also become increasingly dependent upon unreliable income from international student fees. In response to the necessity of seeking increased revenue and new funding sources, our universities have also become more and more corporatized and (arguably) more business facing. Moreover, our university leadership has moved into the 'corporate, executive remuneration' sphere and is visibly influenced and emulative of those corporate,

---

68 Conor King (2021). Education Follows the Big Drivers. Farewell Address to the ATN, reported in CMM, 28th July 2021

69 Half of UK university students think degree is poor value for money. Results from The Higher Education Policy Group Thinktank, Student Survey. Rachel Hall, The Guardian, UK. 21 6 2021

70 Student satisfaction in Australian universities drops to an all-time low. Editorial, The Guardian, Australia. 21/03/2021

71 'Too many graduates, too few jobs…' The Australian, 26th July 2020

72 Althusser, Louis (2014) On the Reproduction of Capitalism: Ideology and Ideological State Apparatuses. Verso UK

profitmaking behaviours typical of commercially competitive global industries.

That old notion of universities being concerned with 'public good' is beginning to wear thin as some university CEOs run chain saws through cherished areas of academic study and staffing levels are minimised in order to shrink salary costs. Since COVID-19, above the surface, numbers of 17,300 tertiary job losses have been cited by Universities Australia[73], but the scale of the bottom portion of this redundancy iceberg is yet to become clear (J. Mienczakowski & G. Whateley, 2021)[74]. The job shedding trend actually commenced long before Covid-19 arrived, and it continues with even more universities moving towards further job losses and restructuring as the pandemic continues (Campus Mail, 5th & 29th July; 2nd August 2021). Beyond COVID-19, another fundamental driver for this job shedding has been continuous high investment in rankings-related research capacities.

By utilising iPod, e, b & hLearning strategies, universities are seeking to further reduce delivery costs. The lockstep relationship that Australian universities have developed with international ranking metrics (which uniformly demand high quality research outputs) is problematic. Research, of course, is globally important but majorly expensive. The suite of cheaper eLearning approaches being adopted during the COVID-19 pandemic is unlikely to be soon jettisoned as universities, as yet, have not identified alternative sources of revenue to equal that which was once provided by international students. When international numbers begin to flow again, it will be some time before universities recover the financial losses of the pandemic. Less costly eLearning approaches will inevitably be in focus for a long time to come.

NON-COMPREHENSIVE PROVIDERS

The value of smaller operations such as UBSS is as much in what they don't offer as well as in what they actually do provide. Non-Comprehensive Providers often specialise in small portfolios of

---

[73] Universities Australia, 3rd February 2021

[74] Mienczakowski, J. & Whateley, G. Ranking addiction: Time to rethink the habit? Campus Review, 16th Feb 2021

profession related degrees. Their academic faculty meet TEQSA and accreditation requirements and have both professional experience and teaching expertise. Their mission is to seek success for their students. Ultimately, they are 'research aware' more than 'research producing'.

This difference in focus (from teaching to research) is critical. The 2020 QILT survey results (determining student satisfaction in learning and teaching) clearly demonstrated that students placed some of the teaching focussed private providers as being the Australian leaders in delivering quality learning experiences. Accordingly, UBSS, along with Bond University, came out at the top of these rankings - with the lowest student satisfaction levels being recorded by some of our most revered Top 100 institutions. This David v Goliath result reflects the potential of the research aligned (but not research-focussed) quality small providers to help students individually fulfil their best potential. It is also within these Non-Comprehensive Provider environments (as demonstrated in the QILT 2020 results) that utilisation, development, and knowhow in bLearning, eLearning and hLearning approaches have become highly effective and student endorsed.

THE MOOC MOVEMENT

The incoming University of Sydney vice-chancellor, Mark Scott, warns of the future online challenge to public universities. In recognising the strengthening position of the US educational technology corporates who recently bought the assets of edX from Harvard and MIT (*part of the MOOC movement*), he points to the potential threat to market share posed by *"....'slick' online course provision offered by growing US corporates such as Coursera and 2U."*[75] Massive Open Online Courses are still a concept under construction, but they hold the potential to radically alter the way in which students from around the world can build and package credits towards a degree award. The strong interest demonstrated in MOOCs is another powerful driver for change. It denotes a potentially huge market seeking alternative forms of access into

[75] Tim Dodd HE Editor. (The Australian July 17-18, 2021)

degree level studies. Again, these future approaches are almost entirely h, b & eLearning in nature.

CONCLUSION

Our current on-campus, F2F expectations will eventually be diminished simply because iPod, Zoom, eLearning, etc. create flexibility and the opportunity for asynchronous study. They reduce the need to travel to a campus. They will provide cheaper pathways for tertiary studies which are open to wider audiences. Smaller entities, such as UBSS, with their eLearning expertise and student focus, can be a reliable bridge between students new to tertiary education and their successful attainment of a degree. As the costs entailed in gaining an on-campus degree inevitably increase, physically attending a large public university will more likely be something you do for your graduate studies.

Emeritus Professor Jim Mienczakowski, Higher Education Consultant

The impact of Coronavirus on international students and education providers in Australia

Rhonda Rowland

INTRODUCTION

In a time of uncertainty and ongoing disruption around the world, this global interruption is having a significant impact on international students in Australia and their education providers. This paper sets out who the international student is, what they bring to the Australian economy and the effects of this crisis on the economy and the community. The implications of the pandemic on this sector will have long term ramifications from both an economic and a social perspective if a new approach to the changes needed is not implemented quickly. Certainly, the education sector is highly motivated to work with the government in building a first-class digital teaching platform with a goal of providing access to courses from anywhere in the world. The hybrid models of the digital classroom and the encouragement of the safe return of the students when the borders have reopened are all part of the reforms needed to keep the balance between domestic and international students in play.

WHO IS THE INTERNATIONAL STUDENT?

The international student is the student who chooses to undertake all or part of their higher education in another country and relocate for that purpose. In Australia, a student must acquire a student visa and enrol in an institution registered to deliver such courses. International students can study at various levels of education, from vocational education and English language courses through to university degrees.

In 2012 the Australian government encouraged an increase in overseas student numbers on the condition that the quantity of places offered to domestic students would not be reduced. Growth in student numbers from this time has almost doubled, with business studies being the most sought after. International students have contributed significantly to the transformation of our cities, added to our economy, and brought cultural interaction into our community. The COVID-19 pandemic effectively halted global travel, and with it, the possibility of international study.

VISAS FOR INTERNATIONAL STUDENTS

Types of student visa

In Australia there are currently 8 types of student visa. They vary from full-time English course visas to Higher Education Sector visas, all the way to Postgraduate Research Sector visas. The impact from the decline in student numbers is substantial and widespread, particularly given the diversity of visas on offer and the mixture of students applying for them. The reputation of Australia as a high-quality education provider in a country that is considered safe only helps if the students can arrive. The migration of students to other countries with equally high standards could mean these countries will become the new beneficiaries of the international student[76].

[76] ICEF Monitor, International Survey of education agents reveals optimism (2021)

Current Visa Numbers

Since the beginning of the pandemic, visa applications from the international student sector have fallen approximately 39%[77]. The numbers continue to fall whilst the borders remain closed. This number will be further exaggerated in the future if the graduating student is not replaced. Forecasting the impact on the numbers becomes quite complicated, with so many foreign students enrolled studying remotely. As the pandemic worsened, many international students returned to their home country and continued their studies from abroad to keep their visas current.

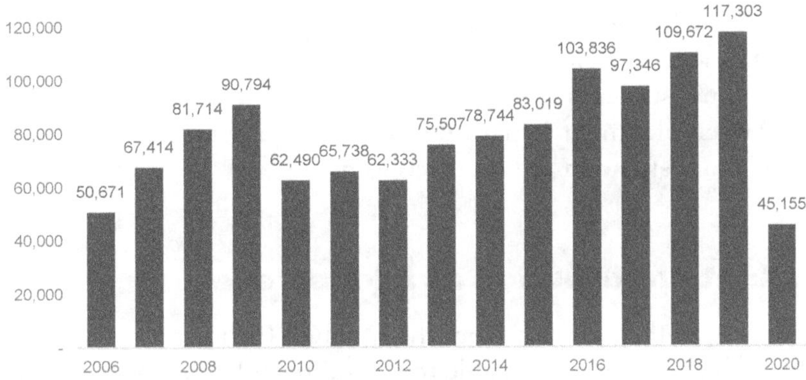

Figure 1 - International student visa applications for April to June (financial quarter 4) 2006 to 2020 - Department of Home Affairs (2020a)

ECONOMIC IMPLICATIONS

The Australian Bureau of Statistics (2020) estimates the contribution from the international educational sector to the Australian economy is around $23 billion in goods and services[78]. The Reserve Bank of Australia stated the contribution of the educational export sector was close to $40 billion in 2019 with $17

---

77 Hurley, P. (2020) Coronavirus and International Students

78 Australian Bureau of Statistics. 2019-2020

billion being from tuition and the balance from the students' living expenditures[79].

Student expenditure

Mitchell Institute research for 2019-2020 shows the contribution of the international students' general expenditure was approximately 70%[80]. Housing and travel are amongst the highest expenditure other than tuition fees. Capital cities attract more of the international student population spend, with most choosing to live close to their education provider, many students needing to supplement their savings with casual employment, and jobs being generally more abundant in the larger cities. With the closure of many of the hospitality venues during the pandemic and with the ongoing lockdowns in the states, the employment situation for international students has become uncertain, the effect of the higher unemployment translating to the decrease in the discretionary spend in the local economy.

Student contribution at a local level

According to the research from the Mitchell Institute, businesses in outer suburbs where affordable rents and reliable transport choices have encouraged a high student population are suffering as students return to their home country[81]. The lack of spending from the extended student population, which includes their friends and family, is placing additional pressure on local neighbourhoods that have become dependent on the student community.

SOCIAL AND WELLBEING IMPLICATIONS

The social and cultural contribution from the international student cannot be dismissed. Their contribution to the internationalisation of the classroom not only benefits the institution where they choose to study, it also adds invaluable wider social acceptance to

[79] RBA Bulletin, December 2020

[80] Hurley, P. (2020) Coronavirus, and the International Student

[81] Hurley, P. (2020) International students vital to the coronavirus recovery

the classroom[82]. International students are acknowledged as more than a student - they are colleagues, friends, neighbours, tenants, and customers. The friendships formed from our open borders to international students broadens our thinking and acceptance of different cultures, adds to our tolerance, and encourages cultural engagement[83].

Risks to the wellbeing of the international student

Some international students have been made to feel unwelcome, racist slurs have occurred, and the stigma associated with some countries where the virus has been dominating have made the international student socially anxious and added to the already high levels of mental stress[84]. For some students, trying to process the new reality and the changes needed to adapt on so many levels is very confronting. Many are dependent on what the campus of their educational institution provides - access to technology, a safe place to study - and questions over a student's ability to afford new living arrangements have surfaced as the pandemic continues.

TRANSFER TO THE DIGITAL PLATFORM

The crisis of the global pandemic brought forward, at great speed, the move to learning via the digital platform. As the closure of the educational learning providers occurred around the world, the need to learn via the internet and other technologies, and the question of best delivery, was fast tracked[85]. Whilst the education sector had online education as an option, it was the face-to-face teaching alongside the interaction within the classroom that was always the preferred model, not just for the student but for the teacher and

---

[82] Hurley, P. (2020) International students vital to the coronavirus recovery
[83] Oanh (Olena) Thi Kim Nguyen & Varsha Devi Balakrishnan (2020) International students in Australia – during and after COVID-19, Higher Education Research & Development
[84] International Education. International students and their mental health and physical safety, p.10
[85] World Economic Forum, The Covid-19 has changed education forever. This is how. April 2020

the administrators as well. Whilst many had believed the rapid move to online learning would result in poor user experience, the transition has been received with more enthusiasm and success as improvements in delivery and efficiency are made[86]. The success of the transition to the online courses and the positive take-up of the chat groups and video meetings, as well as the ease of document sharing, have many believing that both offline and online learning will be the new normal once the pandemic is over. The hybrid model, as it is referred to, is here to stay[87].

Challenges to the digital learning platform

The gap between those from wealthier countries and those from disadvantaged backgrounds and poorer countries, where access to the internet is unreliable, makes the digital platform at times impossible. Mastery of technology, lack of appropriate devices, fields of study that cannot transition to online and the home learning environment can all contribute to challenges faced with online learning[88].

Student engagement and integrity

Whilst online learning and virtual classrooms have been an essential transition, the challenges of engaging the student can be more exaggerated with international students. Language and cultural barriers may leave them out of class discussions, and their ability to understand instruction may contribute to them falling behind. The seriousness of the integrity of their exams can also be questioned, as the temptation to cheat when not in the classroom environment can, under pressure, be seen as an easy option.

Isolation

Social isolation is real and more exaggerated with international students who are already away from family and friends. The

[86] Online Education: Worldwide Status, Challenges, Trends, and Implications
[87] National Education Association, Overview Hybrid Learning Models, 2021
[88] Tertiary Education and Quality Standards Agency, November 2020

inability to meet with the teachers or fellow students can contribute to the overall offshore educational experience.

POLICIES TO SUPPORT THE RETURN OF THE INTERNATIONAL STUDENT

To help kick start Australia's fourth largest export sector, the government announced changes to the granting of the international student visa, allowing students to continue taking classes online whilst living overseas. The public statement that accompanied the changes pushed the rhetoric of "the world class education system with some of the lowest rates of COVID-19 in the world, we want to welcome them back in a safe and measured way when it is safe to do so."[89]

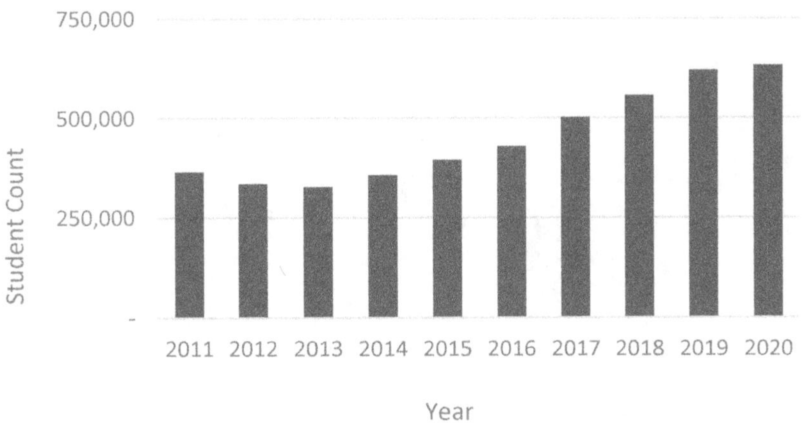

Figure 2 - International students in Australia - Australian Trade and investment Commission, May 2021

[89] Joint Media Release, The Hon Alan Tudge MP, July 2020

INTERNATIONAL STUDENTS ARE AN INTEGRAL PART OF BOTH CAMPUS LIFE AND SOCIETY

International students are an integral part of both campus life and society. The benefits to communities go beyond the education cycle of the student, they enhance our cultural community and bring important social and economic gain to all. Advances in the delivery of the content via digital platforms and the government's encouragement and commitment to the return of the international student post COVID-19 will help support a viable education sector which, in turn, will continue to bring a positive contribution to the national economy.

Rhonda Rowland, Concierge and Professional Staff member, UBSS.

10 things to know about online learning, or otherwise, what do you need to know to teach online?

Anurag Kanwar

INTRODUCTION

Due to the COVID-19 pandemic there has been a shift towards online learning[90]. The traditional mode of delivery - face to face - has been deemed too risky during extended lockdowns and restrictions, given the necessary movement of large numbers of students. As a result, education providers have moved to online and other flexible modes of delivery.

There are ten things to be aware of from a provider point of view –

BUDGET

In any move to online learning, the first issue to consider is what the provider's budget is for the purchase of any specialised equipment. Will the provider be relying on existing IT infrastructure? Some providers have even relied on the academics

[90] *https://www.ubss.edu.au/media/2760/alternate-delivery-modes-for-international-students.pdf* accessed 3 August 2021

themselves for all the IT equipment and software. While this is the cheapest way out, it may not deliver the desired results in terms of the student learning experience[91].

EQUIPMENT

In traditional face to face learning and teaching, a provider usually has a single learning management system. Often, little or no consideration is given to the classroom set up. Online learning (if delivered from the campus) requires a reconfiguration of teaching spaces. Specialised equipment such as interactive whiteboards, tracking cameras, portable microphones are necessary for a professional delivery. One provider converted classrooms into lecture studios to create an optimum learning environment[92]. Note that international students often pay a premium and are likely to be unhappy customers if their online learning experience is substandard.

SUPPORT

What support can be provided to academics and students to facilitate their online learning experience? Is it possible to provide a helpline or chat service or a number so that academics and students may contact each other in the event of an 'outage'? Such support measures are necessary for online learning but come at a significant cost to the provider.

ACADEMICS

Does your academic team understand what it means to teach online? Online teaching requires a certain skill set, not just in

[91] *https://www.ubss.edu.au/articles/2021/may/online-teaching-a-tale-of-two-institutions/* accessed 3 August 2021

[92] *https://www.ubss.edu.au/media/1824/transition-to-online-teaching-and-learning-at-ubss-2020.pdf* accessed 4 August 2021

delivery, but also around how to use equipment. How tech savvy are your academics[93]?

To successfully teach online requires a certain level of technological proficiency. This includes the ability to understand online communication etiquette, how to log in and how to deliver the lectures in a style that is communicative and informed. Staff may need to be trained in such matters prior to the commencement of online delivery.

Prior to any online delivery, academics may need to be provided with detailed training on how to use the technology. This would ensure that expectations regarding behaviour and performance are met. For example, ensuring that the cameras are switched on and microphones are worn and used appropriately tells the student the teachers are prepared.

STUDENTS

Are your students familiar with the learning management system? Can the student even use a computer? Murdoch University[94] experienced some difficulties in recent times, given a large cohort of students were not particularly familiar with the use of computers. It is likely that such students would struggle with online learning.

The other issue to consider is centred on expected behaviours of students whilst learning online. Have these expectations been communicated to the students? This may include such things as keeping the camera on at all times. The provider needs to be aware that perhaps it is not possible for students to keep their camera on for the duration of the class. What work around strategies should be provided to the student to ensure their learning outcomes are met?

---

[93] *https://www.ubss.edu.au/media/2754/online-learning-and-the-organisation.pdf* accessed 3 August 2021

[94] *https://www.abc.net.au/news/2019-10-11/murdoch-university-sues-four-corners-whistleblower/11591520* accessed 3 August 2021

STUDENT AGREEMENTS

International students (those students who hold a valid student visa) are subject to conditions imposed by the ESOS Act 2000 and the National Code[95]. This stipulates the percentage of classes students are permitted to complete online, and that students are required to attend face to face classes[96].

All international students are required to have a Student Agreement which documents the rights and responsibilities of both the student and the provider[97]. Therefore, if a provider changes the mode of delivery, the provider is technically in 'provider default' and the student is entitled to a refund.

The provider must ensure that the student is aware of any change and accepts the change accordingly. Should a student not consent, the provider will be obligated to release the student and any monies paid, as the provider has breached the original agreement and is now in provider default (unable to deliver the original course). It is acknowledged that as of the date of writing, as a result of the pandemic, there is some flexibility with the requirement for face-to-face learning.

ASSESSMENT

The next question to consider is how students are currently assessed. If the unit outline requires particular modes of assessment such as invigilated exams, what are the alternatives? We should also consider that time may need to be given to academics to revamp the unit outlines and assessments. This may mean extra costs for the provider in paying academics for additional course revisions. If students are awarded a grade for class participation, how will this be considered within an online environment? The Course Advisory Committee and/or Academic Board/Senate may need to become

---

95 *https://www.dese.gov.au/esos-framework* accessed 3 August 2021

96 *https://www.dese.gov.au/esos-framework/resources/standard-8-overseas-student-visa-requirements*

97 *https://www.dese.gov.au/esos-framework/resources/standard-3-formalisation-enrolment-and-written-agreements* see Standard 3.

involved in order to provide advice to the academic team on such matters.

POLICIES AND PROCEDURES

All providers have numerous policies and procedures in place to cover issues such as Bullying, Workplace Safety and Grievance Handling. If a provider is moving into the online space, it will need to look carefully at the existing policies and procedures to ensure they are applicable to the online mode. For example, the Bullying Policy will need to address the possibility that bullying can occur through text messages, emails, instant messaging, and other social media platforms. In addition, it is the employer's responsibility to maintain a safe working environment[98]. This would presumably mean informing employees of all hazards in the online workplace. The provider will need to look at whether it has the necessary specialised advice in-house or if there is a need to source an external expert.

STUDENT SERVICES

Providers often pride themselves on offering students a number of 'add on' services coupled with a quality education; these may include workshops, social activities, and a range of other options. In a traditional university model these are important. The question to consider is how these services can be replicated in an online environment. If they cannot, then the provider will need to rethink what 'student services' they can actually deliver. Some providers have moved from traditional student services events to online (virtual) events. Some events include resume writing, interview tips and maintaining a positive outlook during a pandemic. Such online events are of value to the provider and the student, but they can be expensive. These will need to be carefully considered by the provider.

---

[98] *https://www.education.vic.gov.au/school/students/beyond/Pages/dutiesofemployers.aspx* accessed 4 August 2021

FEEDBACK

This is important and sometimes overlooked. How does the provider obtain feedback from the end users on the online experience? The needs and experiences of the student can vary greatly from those of the lecturers/academics. The provider may need to develop a specialised system for recording feedback appropriately and one that, in turn, feeds into organisational changes.

Anurag Kanwar, Director of Compliance and Continuous Improvement, Group Colleges Australia.

Blended learning: a personal, practical perspective

Cyril Jankoff

INTRODUCTION

I facilitate short non-award courses for executives and executive MBA students. I do this locally and overseas. For many years I have embedded Malcolm Knowles' six principles of andragogy in adult education to improve adult learning. In this chapter I will concentrate on my use of blended learning with executive MBA students, starting with a background overview, before ending with an evaluation of my experience with blended learning.

MALCOLM KNOWLES' SIX PRINCIPLES OF ANDRAGOGY

Knowles described andragogy as the art and science of adult learning. His theory can be stated with six assumptions related to the motivation of adult learning[99]: (1) adults need to know why they need to learn something; (2) adults need to build on their experience (including errors); (3) adults have a need to feel responsible for their learning; (4) adults are ready to learn if

[99] Knowles, M., Holton, E., and Swanson, R., The Adult Learner – The Definitive Classic in Adult Education and Human Resource Development, 5 ed 1998, Butterworth-Heinemann, Woburn, MA, USA

learning solves an immediate problem; (5) adults want their training to be problem focused; and (6) adults learn best when motivation comes from within rather than externally. As will be seen below, I use these principles on a day-to-day basis.

SUCCESS IS OFTEN ELUSIVE

In 1981 I commenced a graduate course in Taxation Law. In 1986 Stephen Carty, the head of the law department where I had studied, offered me the opportunity to teach Business Law in the evenings. He said that the full-time lecturers did not want to teach in the evenings. I accepted the offer. I was very motivated. At the end of the first lecture, a delegation comprising a number of students approached Stephen asking for me to be removed as my lecturing was so bad. As luck would have it, Stephen was a very kind man and sat me down and quietly spoke to me about the facts of life in education. Nearly forty years later, embarrassingly, I still vividly recall him looking at me and saying, "Son, you need only use one case as an example and not one hundred…" As I listened, Julius Caesar's 47 BC statement, *veni, vidi, vici* (I came, I saw, I conquered) was in my mind and I thought, 'I came, I taught, and I failed.' However, luck was very much with me as Stephen gave me another chance, and he agreed to mentor me. Had he growled and taken a different approach with me that would have been the end of my teaching career and I would not be writing this chapter.

IMPROVEMENT OVER TIME

Over time I worked hard to learn how to be a better adult educator, but never forgot the vital other side - the adult learner - or counterparty in lawyer talk. Knowles' principles are indelibly etched into my mind, and I use them on a daily basis. I still practise as a solicitor and CPA, advising on business improvement, and do this to keep current and provide my students with interesting and current case studies. My true passion, however, and most of my time now, is focused on adult education through the training of executives and lecturing to executive MBA students at the

Universal Business School Sydney's[100] (UBSS) Executive Delivery MBA. It took a long time, but I now feel comfortable delivering to executives, and I prefer this category of student. I have received two UBSS Executive Dean Teaching Awards (2020 and 2021).

THE UBSS EXECUTIVE DELIVERY MBA

At UBSS there is an MBA that caters for two markets. The one for international students tends to be for younger students mainly from overseas, and the Executive Delivery MBA tends to be for older domestic students with more high-level work experience. My focus is on the latter. Senior Management at UBSS has worked hard to make the Executive Delivery MBA as engaging and as valuable an experience as possible for the students. This is done in a number of ways.

It is a fact of life that the typical Executive Delivery MBA student is in a very vulnerable position in their life: working hard to prove themselves to get promotions and increased salaries, and then going home to more work in the form of a young family. The holy grail would be to find a better, and less abrasive way, to complete executive education, such as an MBA, and obtain an education that is practical, with key learnings that will "stick".

The UBSS model is designed around a subject being taught in a CBD six times per year, that is, once every two months. Given there are 16 units in the MBA, the program, then, can be completed in fewer than three years - on a part-time basis.

The typical subject is run as follows: *the printed/ online materials* would be provided at the beginning of the month, about four weeks before the face-to-face class. The class at the end of the month is three consecutive days - a Friday, Saturday, and a Sunday - and is held at an up-market hotel, currently the Primus Hotel in Sydney and the Windsor Hotel in Melbourne. After the third face to face class, the students have two weeks to complete their major assessment, and then two weeks to rest before the next subject commences. Minor assessments occur during the three faces to

100 *www.UBSS.edu.au*

face days, including quizzes and short answer questions. These are answered using mobile devices.

The students are prescribed reading in the four weeks prior to class. In the first week they are to read up on the first face to face day's classes, then in the second week, the second face to face day's classes, and the third week, the third face to face day's classes. In the fourth week they are to summarise the prior three weeks and complete a number of activities.

Students have a one hour Zoom session one night per week with their lecturer. There are two reasons for this. The first is that it allows students the opportunity to discuss any issues in relation to the subject and to review set activities and case studies, and this means students can go through the key principles in that week's content. The second reason is that the teacher can ensure that all students are adhering to the timelines, all the while, keeping them engaged. This active review is preferred over a passive review comprising an email with a lecturer's suggestion to complete certain reading and activities. The lecturer contacts those who did not attend (if any) to briefly speak with them to ensure they are not falling behind.

Each of the three faces to face teaching days has four sessions, totalling twelve sessions for the three days. If the MBA was for some reason taught over twelve weeks, then each session would represent a week, with more materials, activities, case studies added where necessary. The four daily sessions are: the first before the morning break; the second before lunch; the third before the afternoon break; and the fourth is before the end of the day. Each session is approximately one and a half hours in length, with thirty minutes for each of the morning and afternoon breaks and one hour for lunch. This allows plenty of time to rest, network, speak about the assessment and consume food and beverages. Each session is based on Knowles' principles and comprises three parts: an introduction to the theory, one or more activities and a review of the materials. In some classes there may be assessment requirements, often a quiz or short answer questions.

In each subject an industry expert is invited to speak, and this normally occurs in the tenth session, that is, the session before lunch on the last day. Students are asked in advance to suggest topics, including those that may cover their chosen areas for the final major assessment. The guest speaker is requested to keep the discussion practical and is encouraged to stay for lunch and mingle with the students. Any faculty member who happens to be available on the day is invited to attend the presentation, meet the students, and have lunch with all present.

Clearly, there needs to be a focus on learning and teaching. In relation to learning, it is important to remember that the learners are customers. We all know that this is something that is not always remembered, especially in the prestigious universities. Learners are to be treated with respect and in a business-like manner. Male lecturers are expected to dress in business suits and ties, and women with the equivalent business attire. Lecturer failure to attend an agreed class is treated very seriously. Expertise with the subject matter is mandatory, as is experience in teaching executives.

In many cases COVID-19 has been, and it seems will be for some time, a major disruptor. Considering the above, however, it is my experience that COVID-19 is more of an irritant. This is because the classes can easily be taught online, either over the three weeks, or over the weekend, again, online.

BLENDED LEARNING: A PRACTICAL PERSPECTIVE

Professor Andrew West noted (Chapter 2) that Bonk and Graham defined "blended learning systems" as learning systems that "combine face to face (F2F) instruction with computer mediated instruction."[101] I have been involved with MBA courses for thirty years now, both as a student and as a lecturer, and as an undergraduate lecturer for five years before that. My teaching has occurred in many formats, including F2F, hybrid, distance learning and blended learning. I consider that the above UBSS blended learning model is advantageous for many reasons, not least that it provides a way to balance three viciously competitive components: study, work, and family. After teaching the UBSS blended model for two years, I wish my own MBA was undertaken in such a blended learning way, as mine was very difficult due to high study,

[101] Bonk, C and Graham, C (Eds.). (2006). Handbook of blended learning: Global Perspectives, local designs. San Francisco, CA: Pfeiffer Publishing

work, and family expectations. I believe I would have learned more quickly, more easily, and retained knowledge and enjoyed it more. It is my opinion that for the learner, blended learning allows for more engagement and satisfaction, with a reduced dropout rate. On the other side, blended learning provides the opportunity for the lecturer to be more engaged and achieve more job satisfaction, with a decrease in the number of learners leaving the profession or the higher education provider.

These positives can only benefit the higher education provider. I am very much in favour of blended learning, and strongly believe it has considerable advantage over other types of learning, including hybrid and online learning.

Associate Professor Cyril Jankoff, Programs Director, UBSS Melbourne CBD Campus.

Interview style guest presentations that enhance learning

Art Phillips

One hundred per cent face to face (F2F) learning and delivery in higher education is becoming more of a memory than a continued reality. Online learning and delivery have existed for quite some time and has now become essential during the 2020/2021 COVID-19 crisis, especially here in Australia. Once the crisis subsides, these two forms of delivery will merge into what has been tagged 'hybrid' delivery - providing learning choices that the student will make to best suit their lifestyle.

As Shannon Flynn notes[102]: 'Hybrid learning is a reliable method of teaching for higher education. It combines online and in-person learning as some students watch virtually and others go to the classroom. Hybrid learning can improve the flexibility and customization of classes, the accessibility of learning and the use of tools during courses. This experience facilitates an all-around better teaching and learning environment for educators and students in higher education. Though it has been an option for several years, the (COVID-19) pandemic has emphasized its importance and functionality. It's more essential than ever that educators find a way to connect students while keeping everyone physically safe.'

---

102 *https://www.cybintsolutions.com/3-benefits-of-hybrid-learning/*

Hybrid teaching may involve synchronous and asynchronous learning activities. Synchronous learning is interactive, two-way online or distance education that happens in real time with a teacher, whereas asynchronous learning occurs virtually online and through prepared resources, without real-time teacher-led interaction.

The greatest task in all forms of education is how to best engage the student to increase learning absorption, and for myself, I much prefer *synchronous* teaching, as learning outcomes are much stronger.

The University of Colorado Denver website[103] notes: '**The Advantages of Synchronous Teaching**:

1. Immediate personal engagement between students and instructors, which may create greater feelings of community and lessen feelings of isolation.
2. More responsive exchanges between students and instructors, which may prevent miscommunication or misunderstanding.'

As we know from life experiences, we learn best when we are drawn to something that provides strong relatability. It is, therefore, essential for the lecturer to know how to read their students, and to provide interesting and entertaining content delivery - and preferably 'live'. I am convinced that spontaneous reaction and interaction with the content topic and with the student at that precise intuitive and interactive moment is essential for students to experience and absorb the deepest learning.

It is essential that the lecturer shows care for their students, by enriching them with meaningful learning experiences, such as, real-life business stories to heighten enthusiasm and passion for the student. This type of learning content is priceless.

I also believe that the lecturer now needs to be a performer rather than just a teacher -delivering content, not unlike a television presenter, capturing and holding interest, speaking clearly with enthusiasm in the delivery of the story, and providing information that sticks with the viewer.

---

[103] *https://clas.ucdenver.edu/working-remotely/faculty/pedagogy-time-disruption/advantages-and-disadvantages-synchronous-and-asynchronous-teaching*

The University of Washington[104] (USA) notes: 'Research has demonstrated that engaging students in the learning process increases their attention and focus, motivates them to practise higher-level critical thinking skills, and promotes meaningful learning experiences. Instructors who adopt a student-centred approach to instruction increase opportunities for student engagement, which then helps everyone more successfully achieve the course's learning objectives.'

In one of my articles, '*Never lose the moment*'[105], I note that '**Change is essential** - the transition from face to face to online teaching, stemming from the global pandemic of COVID-19, has provided fresh visionary platforms for creatives, academics, and business entrepreneurs. Delivery of learning materials in the online environment cannot remain the same as classroom delivery, as lecturers now need to grab hold of each and every moment and nurture their student audience with continual engagement through heightening interest, introducing relevant surprise events, and allowing more fluid interaction through increased student participation.'

The institution where I lecture has been using guest lecturer presentations for a few years, and these are a wonderful tool to value-add to student learning, whether online or in a hybrid teaching environment. In using this method, however, the guest presenter needs to be completely comfortable operating the audio and visual equipment in the delivery classroom which interfaces with 'blackboard collaborate'[106] - our delivery platform. It is best that the presenter understands how to fly that model plane safely (by way of analogy), usually requiring some flight training, or there will be mishaps and accidents along the route. As the guest presenters are not usually staff members, they would be unfamiliar with the tech tools being used.

So, in 2021, I implemented a highly effective approach with the use of 'interview style guest presentations', where I, as the lecturer, act as the interviewer, interviewing a successful entrepreneurial guest as the feature performer.

---

104 *https://teaching.washington.edu/topics/engaging-students-in-learning/*
105 *https://www.ubss.edu.au/never-lose-the-moment/*
106 *https://www.blackboard.com/en-apac/teaching-learning/collaboration-web-conferencing/blackboard-collaborate*

This style of offering is unique to the classroom, as it is more in the vein of a fireside chat[107] along the lines of a television host and guest, rather than a TEDx-talk format[108]. The fireside chat interview style events take place in the lecture room which is fitted out not unlike a television set for the event, with a comfortable 2-seater leather lounge (for the guest) and a 1-seater matching leather chair (for the interviewer) with coffee table in front of the lounge set. The backdrop image, behind the set, is a wall projected view of our stunning Sydney Harbour Bridge and Opera House, creating an attractive tourism type feel, an aid to advertising the impeccable location of Sydney, Australia - as most of the institute's cohort are from overseas.

The set design in the classroom provides an inviting and homey environment, like a living room television talk show. This interview style format allows students to feel more in the moment and to interact more comfortably during the class event, thereby invigorating student participation.

I consider and engage the best suited business entrepreneurs to interview, then set class dates that coincide well with the subject unit content. I then conduct thorough background research about the guest and prepare the flow of questions for the interview. These questions are designed to benefit learning content with discussions about their business stories and career experience. I liaise with the guest ahead of the event date so that they are comfortable with the questions, and for the guest to better understand how the event will be framed.

Interview style guest presentations enhance learning in the classroom because they are spontaneous, whilst at the same time are focused with a clear plan. This method helps hold viewer interest. The interviewer is the producer, the editor, and the notional pilot, steering the ship according to the swells and currents of the moment. The interviewer needs to feel and understand the moment and move swiftly and accurately in the interview chair by delivering and producing clear, open, and comfortable conversation with the guest.

---

[107] *https://medium.com/@Slidoapp/why-and-how-to-organize-fireside-chats-at-your-event-74ee55e90334*

[108] *https://www.ted.com/watch/tedx-talks*

With this interview style format, the guest does not have much preparation to consider, as the interviewer will be the active event 'juggler'. The guest, having been pre-informed of the questions that they have agreed to, can relax, and go with the flow as long as the interviewer is taking charge and never losing the moment. It is also important for the interviewer to entice the students from time to time during the interview to help get them excited, giving them something to relate to. This will maximize engagement during the Q&A element, in the last fifteen minutes of the event. Care for, and engagement of, the students is critical in teaching. Interaction along the way from the students is encouraged, if online, via the 'chat box' and open mic when called upon.

A friendly, warm, and entertaining environment is sought from this fireside chat interview format, designed to benefit learning outcomes by providing an interesting backdrop, feel and production style for a more engaged learning experience. I also take on the role, at the institution, to arrange interview style presentations for other subjects in other lecturers' classrooms. The fireside chat style events have been well-received with positive responses and outcomes from numerous student surveys.

Michael Roberto[109], Trustee Professor of Management at Bryant University, previously faculty member at Harvard Business School, notes: 'Students form judgments about their courses and their instructors within the opening moments of a class. When teachers fail to hook students' attention up front, engagement remains a struggle for the rest of the semester. To me, engagement is also about showing the students you care. An engaged student Is an inspired one.'

The interview event is recorded and then forms a part of the institute's video publication series, a library series of scholarship which can be re-used and shared across various learning platforms and subjects. Additionally, these publications promote continued learning for our alumni and other scholars.

The video productions also allow for short 'one off edits' of select 'single questions and answers' to use as 'podcast titbits' for social media posts, therein creating a 'library' for lecturers to grab any short audio file relevant to their topic to intersperse in their

[109] *https://hbsp.harvard.edu/inspiring-minds/engaging-students-on-the-first-day-and-every-day*

teaching. Lecturers can use these short audio files of a single question and answer to value-add to their power point slides as snappy audiophile learning snippets.

A few months ago, I produced a one-hour interview event with special guest, Frank Caruso of Caruso's Natural Health, for my class: Entrepreneurship Report. I aligned this event with the start of the marketing section of the subject as I felt his story would help propel student thinking about the business that they had created for the class assessments. Frank has a wealth of experience which would aid the students on how to think intelligently about how to promote their product and brand in the global marketplace.

The Caruso event included a history of how the Caruso business began with the focus on innovation and development of his brand and product range. We looked at Frank's life story and discussed how he introduces new products into the line and looked at an analysis of changes in his business over the years. We discussed marketing and distribution channels where Frank shared advice to newcomers in developing a business start-up. Frank discussed his '10 principles to success in business'. The event was well received, achieved great reviews, and can be viewed at the following weblink:

https://www.kaltura.com/index.php/extwidget/preview/partner_id/3091243/uiconf_id/46604333/entry_id/1_vekhtxk2/embed/iframe?

As a lecturer, I very much want my students to be completely engrossed in the subject content I am delivering, where I am continually conscious of what their impression might be from what they are seeing and hearing. I use direct examples from my own businesses that align nicely to the subject learning content. This provides strong passion coming from my delivery and helps the student better understand the practical purpose of the content - something they can easily grab and comprehend which has clear reasoning. I show them a lot of what I do in business - how I do it - and discuss results, good and not so good. Real life business stories are essential for a lecturer to deliver to students, along with academic content.

Adjunct Professor Art Phillips, Director of the UBSS Centre for Entrepreneurship. He is a four-time recipient of the UBSS 'Executive Dean Award for Outstanding Commitment to Teaching and Learning' - postgraduate level.

VCE in China: A case study

Tom O'Connor

INTRODUCTION

This paper is a study of the response of a transnational secondary program to COVID-19 and the need to adopt and adapt an online learning methodology.

CONTEXT

As Head of Transnational Education at a Victorian secondary school, I am responsible for the delivery of the Victorian Certificate of Education offshore in seven schools across China. This is a secondary school program over the last two and a half years of high school, consisting of a one-semester Gateway program followed by Years 11 and 12 and the VCE examinations at the end of Year 12. Subjects, typically English, but in some cases, Mathematics and Physics, are taught by a combination of "foreign" teachers from countries other than China, predominantly Chinese teachers with good English language skills. It is the normal secondary setting with teachers and students attending a number of classes across the school day. Mentors based in Melbourne, who work predominantly online with teachers, support these teachers.

As other authors (Whateley[110], Mienczakowski[111], Chanda[112], 2021) note, online learning has been available in higher education in a variety of forms, however, because of the duty of care and supervisory responsibilities of secondary education, it has only ever been an ancillary function, used in the ever-increasing administrative requirements of schooling.

EARLY DAYS

The Lunar New Year Festival in January 2020 saw Chinese and foreign teachers and students travel domestically and internationally. A virus producing flu-like symptoms had appeared in Wuhan and began appearing all over China. As COVID-19 spread, the Chinese lockdown was swift and total. Schools were told quite quickly that they would not be opening at the end of this holiday. Foreign teachers found themselves trapped in their home countries from Jamaica to Poland. Chinese teachers and students were locked into their apartments. We were committed to continuing the VCE program for which parents had paid, so here in Melbourne, we were confronted with having to deliver a "classroom experience" online. And we had a week to do it. This issue was not unique, as Rowland[113] (2021) notes, "As the closure of the educational learning providers happened around the world, the need to learn via the internet and other technologies and the question of best delivery was fast tracked."

There were a number of constraints to negotiate. First, Chinese students do not use laptops but smartphones instead. This was an advantage as not every apartment in China has good quality internet access and phone access is generally quite good. This was a disadvantage in that lessons and interaction had to be geared towards a small screen environment. A classroom became thirty separate bedrooms across each city where the program operated. The software platform had to be one which operated as a smartphone app for the receiver, and a laptop-based program for

---

110 *https://www.ubss.edu.au/media/2760/alternate-delivery-modes-for-international-students.pdf*

111 *https://www.ubss.edu.au/media/2759/future-experience.pdf*

112 *https://www.ubss.edu.au/media/2695/the-efficacy-of-online-studies.pdf*

113 *https://www.ubss.edu.au/media/2761/impact-of-coronavirus.pdf*

the teacher. Also, China has a system of extensive filters on incoming internet data. The "Great Firewall of China" and its banning of all Google products limited the choices. The nature of secondary education and the pedagogy of the VCE are built around an interactive, collaborative view of education and this had to be preserved as far as possible. For example, one assessment task is an oral presentation to the class. Our delivery mode and software choice had to accommodate this, and we were delivering to over 500 students.

Our agent and partner in the offshore project, Mr. Gary Li, has the offices of his AIDE Education group company in Collins Street, Melbourne. He offered his premises and support - so quite quickly we established two rooms as "studios" from which we could operate as virtual classrooms. Along with a camera, microphone and high-speed internet connection, each room had a whiteboard to allow teachers to operate in a familiar environment. The central location meant that teaching staff who lived all over Melbourne could easily travel to these studios. Gary also assisted in getting the "ClassIn" software, a Chinese platform that allowed us to avoid issues with communicating in China. Staff from AIDE conducted training in the program for teachers using the platform, and online teaching began in early March and continued for fourteen weeks until the Chinese summer break.

EXPANDING HORIZONS

While teaching is the core component of the program, other aspects had become integral to its operation. An annual conference has been held every year over the last decade and has grown in stature and significance over the years, attracting politicians and academics from Australia and China. Typically, all teachers, mentors and senior leadership met in a different Chinese city each year. Day one was spent listening to keynote speakers and engaging with expert panel discussions. Days two and three involved all teachers in particular subject areas planning and sharing resources and strategies. There are also social events that reinforce existing relationships and build new ones.

The planning group, having realized that the Conference would have to be virtual, decided to try and preserve as much of its structure as possible. By chance, the Conference fell in between lockdowns and there would be an opportunity for limited gatherings at venues in both countries. RMIT donated its Storey Hall for use in Melbourne, while the Chinese gathered at a hotel in Shanghai. This required more sophisticated technology and each venue was set up with a large cinema-sized video screen, multiple cameras, microphones, and a control panel with the capacity to manage the different media being used, including live interpreting in two languages. The opening day included a recorded message from the Victorian Minister for Education, James Merlino, who had previously attended the conference in China, live keynote addresses from Victorian Government Business Office Commissioner in Shanghai and Minister Counsellor for Education, Brooke Hartigan, from the Australian Embassy in Beijing and Chinese educational academics. Perhaps the most arresting innovation was a panel discussion with four participants in Melbourne and two in Shanghai. The cameras synchronized the visuals, so each venue saw six participants on stage. Another interesting aspect was a "Drinks Party" held at the end of the day to honour the tradition of the Conference dinners. Participants in both venues enjoyed food and drink and shared COVID-19 "war stories" across the big screen.

The following two days were devoted to online planning and resource sessions. A particular interest of the Chinese teachers was observing a demonstration class by exemplary teachers. The electronic format allowed for a new approach to this component. An English class by an excellent teacher in Melbourne was recorded. Through editing, various sections of the class were separated and the pedagogical techniques were highlighted, and Chinese subtitles were added. The video was shown to teachers with mentors online to answer questions and add live comments to the session. The feedback about this was extremely positive.

QUALITY ASSURANCE

The Victorian Curriculum and Assessment Authority is the government body that oversees the conduct of the VCE and has regulatory requirements, particularly around assessment. As

Rowland[114] (2021) rightly observes, the "seriousness of the integrity of their exams can also be questioned, as the temptation to cheat can, under pressure, be seen as an easy option." Exam supervisors represent the frontline that guarantees the integrity of the exam processes. Supervisor training has been a face-to-face exercise conducted annually by the Melbourne school staff and VCAA representatives who normally travel to China to audit exam processes, observing and reporting on the supervisors.

Online training in this case needed to have a live interface section as well as content to which supervisor staff could refer as needed. Using the VCAA manual, a step-by-step recording of the complete supervision process from the arrival of the exam materials at the school until they are handed to the courier for return to Australia was produced. In this case, the content was the major element, so a mock exam was created, and video recorded. Chinese sub-titles were incorporated as was an "index" showing at what time-point in the video various sections were undertaken. This made later referencing much easier. Initially, an online meeting with all supervisors and school staff in Melbourne was arranged and the video was viewed together. This gave the supervisors the chance to ask questions. From there, the Chinese supervisors could keep the video with them, even as they worked through the actual preparation and supervision process. To date, there have been no reported instances of cheating, nor do the statistical analyses of results by VCAA indicate any anomalous grades. So, it is possible to say that this method of training has been successful.

The three experiences described here illustrate the adaptability of the online model.

- The first that sought to mirror the face-to-face experience worked within its limits. The challenge here is to sustain student engagement over extended periods and match the social benefits that accompany schooling; however, the extensive online "life" of modern students has helped with this.
- The second model of a 50/50 hybrid model was very successful, and the benefits of this format will be

114 *https://www.ubss.edu.au/media/2761/impact-of-coronavirus.pdf*

incorporated into future conferences, even if they once again have a large physical gathering of people.

- The third model shows the advantages of online training and could prove to be superior in cost and effectiveness for highly specific and targeted education.

Online teaching and learning offer opportunities as an important tool in modern education at all levels. The experiences of the last eighteen months have tested all those involved and shown the adaptability of organizations and individuals. History demonstrates that large-scale health crises of the past have produced social change. It will be interesting to observe the changes that take place because of this moment in history.

Adjunct Professor Tom O'Connor, Fellow of the UBSS Centre for Scholarship and Research

Online assessment in a digital world

Jotsana Roopram

INTRODUCTION

The COVID-19 pandemic has reshaped online learning and assessment in higher education. At the start of the pandemic, Higher Education Institutions (HEIs) focused primarily on transferring their academic content to digital form. The focus of some institutions was not on a purposeful academic approach aimed at developing effective and sustainable teaching and learning methods, but rather on expediency and the retention of student numbers during the unprecedented crisis. Institutional response times to the pandemic outweighed student capacity to catch up with the rapidly changing digital world, the risk of falling behind enormous. This is particularly relevant with regard to online assessment, where effective strategies were needed to transfer assessments, particularly final examinations, from the conventional learning environment to an adequate and appropriate online format.

The development of students' technical skills, alongside the organisation's investment in robust technological infrastructure, was required to ensure a seamless experience for both students and institutions. The issue of whether faculty were, and are, being prepared and trained adequately to develop suitable online assessments also requires further consideration.

The concept of online assessment was introduced out of necessity at the start of the pandemic and, at first, resulted in some HEIs making use of the Learning Management System (LMS) for open book exams and quizzes, while others explored remote proctoring software. Remote proctoring software provides an added layer of academic integrity to online assessment and its successful use is highly dependent on a number of factors - mostly, students preparing sufficiently for the examination by completing a practice exam, and students having the required technology to successfully access and complete the exam in varied settings and from multiple locations, including worldwide.

STUDENT CHALLENGES

At UBSS, we recently completed the last round of final exams (end of Trimester 2) using remote proctoring software for the first time, with a small sample of students in an undergraduate program. This new experience shed light on a range of factors to consider, including whether remote proctoring software should be used on a larger scale in future final assessments.

Let us consider, then, remote proctoring software requires specific internet connectivity in order to complete an exam. A significant number of UBSS students are currently abroad and completing their studies from their home countries, that is, offshore. Depending on their locations, the reliability of their internet connection has an impact on their ability to successfully navigate this new and sometimes daunting process of undertaking their final assessment online for the trimester with an interface with the proctoring software. Access to fast and reliable internet connection is key to not only having a stress-free online study experience but is necessary for the final assessment process as well. The issue of access is also relevant to students in Australia, perhaps living in shared spaces, most often with shared internet facilities.

Despite regular communication sent to students prior to the exam as well as a survey on the technical requirements distributed early in the trimester (designed to determine whether they had the required software and hardware for the remote proctored exams), issues still arose during the examination process. There was also an expectation of students to have developed a certain level of technical prowess, given that they have been functioning in a digital world for some time – particularly in the past year - and that they have quickly learnt how to navigate self-regulated learning and on-demand content, consumed at their own pace.

What we actually discovered, from the pilot round of remote proctored exams, was a low level of digital readiness[115] or gap in the students' rudimentary understanding of technology - there are some students who are uncomfortable and inept with technology, so the technological requirements of remote proctored assessment was intimidating for them from the very outset. For these students, the pressure of an online final assessment, together with the possibility of technology failing them on the day, was a genuine fear many of them faced.

Another challenge that plays a significant role in student success in online assessment is the language barrier. While this is not unusual for international students, it directly impacts on the time taken to resolve exam-related or technical issues faced by students, in an already time-sensitive situation.

Online assessment can also be more challenging for students, especially if they are completing assessments at home and must contend with situations that are not conducive to taking exams, such as, family in shared living spaces and other living arrangements that may impede their ability to effectively take exams.

Shared devices or no devices raises another set of questions and issues. Does online learning actually bridge the access gap for students who may not have access to the required technology and internet connectivity, or are unable to afford these during a pandemic? Most, if not all, students have been financially impacted by the lockdowns in Australia and/or by the financial ramifications of the pandemic in their home countries. This has played and will play a vital role in students acquiring the recommended devices needed for online study and assessment.

---

[115] Handel, M., Stephan, M, Glaser-Zikuda, M., Kopp, B., Bedenlier, S. & Ziegler, A. (2020). Digital readiness and its effects on higher education students' socio-emotional perceptions in the context of the COVID-19 pandemic. *https://www.tandfonline.com/doi/full/10.1080/15391523.2020.1846147*

THE FUTURE OF ONLINE ASSESSMENT

Given that online assessment will most likely remain a part of higher education for the foreseeable future, a few areas need to be explored further. Should the grade for an entire trimester of study come down to one final assessment? Does the design of the assessment approach in higher education require review and more attention[116]? Is the concept of a final examination an outdated approach to assessment in a new age? Would multiple application-based assessments throughout the trimester be better suited to an online student in the current climate? Could multi-assessment approaches reduce technology-related stress for students by providing them with more than one opportunity to obtain a final grade and allow faculty to intervene earlier to help students progress? Will multi-assessment approaches also increase student engagement and relieve them of the added pressure of the dependence on one final exam to pass a course?[117]

Frequent assessments can reduce distractions and improve student engagement. Early academic intervention is possible with the multi-assessment approach. Indeed, the ultimate goal of improving overall progression and reducing attrition could be achieved too.

Assistant Professor Jotsana Roopram, Deputy Dean (Student Experience), UBSS.

---

[116] Alsadoon, H. (2021). Challenges of deploying online exams. *https://lumenpublishing.com/journals/index.php/rrem/article/download/3439/2916/13320*

[117] Chanda, A. (2021). The Efficacy of Online Studies: Addressing the Student Dilemma. *https://www.ubss.edu.au/media/2695/the-efficacy-of-online-studies.pdf*

The Benefits of the Blended Learning Method

Sam Sorace

INTRODUCTION

I am currently enrolled in the UBSS Executive MBA course which embraces the blended learning method. This method of learning has enabled me to undertake further study while maintaining a work and life balance.

In today's education environment, various digital learning platforms are gaining popularity. More recently, as the world deals with a global pandemic, using the latest technological advances has become essential. Indeed, it seems blended learning will increasingly allow students to obtain the required knowledge virtually and with greater flexibility. The purpose of this paper is to explore the blended learning method and the benefits it provides for individuals who work full-time, have a family, and have limited free time.

BLENDED LEARNING METHOD EXPLAINED

No longer is the traditional method of delivery - from teacher to student in a classroom setting - the only way one can access and undertake further study. First, it is necessary to decide what exactly is meant by the blended learning method. Although the name suggests that this framework is a combination of approaches, it is important to establish where the border between traditional and fully digital learning lies and which techniques come into play. In practice, the variety of techniques is realised through sessions of personal interaction with the instructor and creating a particular platform for self-study[118]. Structured learning, characterised by personal interactions, is combined with the freedom to choose the pace at which one will work independently via a digital platform.

The blended learning method aims to reach the largest possible audience. Compared to digital learning alone, the combination method provides more rigor, structure, and ultimately allows for increased efficiency. Despite specific difficulties in implementing such a method, blended learning makes it possible to offer programmes much more effectively and conveniently to many groups. The blended model also encourages individuals to adapt to different categories of people.

The process of delivering an education will vary depending on the percentage of the traditional approach and the percentage of the distance approach. Whilst one of the most popular methods of delivery remains face-to-face - primarily based on the traditional approach - the addition of technologies provides learners with the opportunity to control the pace of individual learning. As such, the teacher's role includes conducting offline intensives, offering a deeper study of the material, providing feedback and practice, all the while, using the online component. Undoubtedly, this method has many advantages, however, it can be especially useful for working family people with a lack of spare time.

While for students, educational activity is their main occupation, those embarking on further study must pay attention to other things, for example, work and family. Most significantly, then, the blended learning method can be beneficial since such education, in the first place, saves people time[119]. A significant part of the training is carried out on a distance basis, and so, students can acquire the knowledge they need at their own pace during a selected period of time. In addition, it would seem, many topics rich in terminology that must be carefully studied are much more

---

[118] *https://elmlearning.com/blended-learning-everything-need-know/*

[119] *https://www.edgepointlearning.com/blog/benefits-of-blended-learning/*

easily examined and learnt independently, away from a classroom. Traditional classes take up much more time as there is a need to travel to and from the place of study. Certainly, the blended learning method means the time spent on a lesson with an instructor is minimised, even if the intensity of the sessions is increased. Learners, therefore, when together with the teacher, do not spend time on what they can manage in their own time.

TIME SAVING AND COST REDUCTION

An advantage of adopting the blended learning model is saving not only time but money. The two concepts are firmly related, as courses of longer duration typically cost more. As such, offline intensives with a teacher are held less often, the teacher is paid accordingly, their effectiveness greater, allowing one to cost save. Online training is more appealing and convenient since learners are required to pay much less for using one of the many platforms and readily available resources. If the cost is shared or paid in full by the student's employer, there is a further reduction in cost - if not, a full reimbursement - to the student. The cost saving factor is significant for people with a family and, within this context, a shared budget. How ever useful it may be, education should not jeopardise the existing order of things and the established way of life in the family. Therefore, the less a family member is required to spend on further study - and time away from home - the more the family can benefit from it.

COMFORT FACTOR

Further to this, the attractiveness of the blended learning method for the aforementioned group of people lies with the comfort factor. It is important to note here, practice shows that some people are more inclined to work independently online, while for others, the strict order of the live conference is essential. Usually, attitudes towards learning depend on personal qualities and the habitual educational style that the individual has experienced throughout their life. For example, a person educated in a traditional setting may feel less comfortable facing the demand for online-only learning, accelerated during a global pandemic when lockdowns are in place. That noted, the blended method can make working people feel quite comfortable, regardless of their inclinations. Since participation in such educational programs can be an additional stressful load for busy people, providing them with an extra level of comfort means, for example, a more familiar environment is not only welcome but vital.

In addition, blended learning may be more appealing due to the pacing of work. In the same way that some people prefer traditional teaching to distance learning, for some individuals, it may take more time to study, for others, less. Imposing the same program with time constraints on all students seems only to guarantee that certain group members will fail. The blended method allows one to go through most of the educational process independently, at the pace necessary for an individual, in line with personal preferences. Furthermore, such flexibility allows for more efficient scheduling which is especially beneficial for people with little free time. Finally, blended learning is especially effective in complex technical contexts requiring a precise approach to information. Professionals in this field can gradually learn, for example, a programming language, disassembling the elements of syntax using examples, and then consolidate with the instructor.

EFFICIENT AND PRODUCTIVE

A final factor which tells of the attributes of blended learning is the efficiency and productivity it encourages. When starting any educational course, people strive to get a result with the gaining of new knowledge and skills that can be applied either in the current work context or in a new job. Traditional education, in this case, can be highly ineffective in terms of the time required to gain knowledge and obtain a diploma. More dynamic and flexible courses are often much more beneficial in practice. The blended learning method provides a unique opportunity to learn and immediately test new approaches in a secure environment. In addition, it is the combination of preliminary online learning with the subsequent intensive consolidation of knowledge that promises the most outstanding efficiency. A variety of approaches allows one to reach the largest audience by addressing the needs and preferences of a significant number of people. For those already employed in a full-time job who have responsibilities and insufficient free time, the effectiveness of actions, indeed, application of knowledge is essential, and so, this method of learning is ideal for them.

The blended learning mode of delivery is one of the most preferable and most effective for the group of persons central to this discussion paper. The existing combination of factors - saving time and money; ensuring comfortable conditions; the ability to adjust pace of work; the overall effectiveness of the approach - makes this educational method extremely attractive. Given the complexity of combining education, work, and family, it is necessary to be particularly careful when choosing an education model. Thanks to the advantages proposed here, one should feel confident that blended learning interferes with the existing order of affairs as little as possible. Blended learning allows people to effectively combine all types of activities while gaining knowledge and furthering personal development.

Sam Sorace, Fellow of the UBSS Centre for Entrepreneurship, currently enrolled in the UBSS Executive MBA program – delivered in a blended mode.

Learning in the time of Corona

Lauren Whateley

INTRODUCTION

There are few terms in the current English language as fearful as 'COVID-19' - *final notice, random breathalyser…audience participation.* COVID-19 has escalated into the great Goliath of the past eighteen months, and the battle continues, as we, the every-man turned David, fight to regain control and quality of life.

Love in the Time of Cholera (García Márquez, 1985) is a gripping romance set in northern Colombia in the early years of the 20th century which explores how love, like a disease, has ravaged the protagonist defenceless, his sickness comparable to cholera. If I were to put pen to paper and write my own version - *Learning in the Time of Corona* - it would detail my romantic long walks to the study and the fridge, in between Zoom calls, as I yearn for the freedom of the old world (circa 2018). This would be a far less gripping read, and no Nobel-winner, I assure you.

COMMUNICATION FROM MY UNIVERSITY

Just as COVID-19 has ravaged the landscape of our socio-cultural world, so, too, has it wreaked havoc on the fabric of our education system - poking holes in and popping buttons on our tidy and ordered way of learning. The first correspondence I received from my university last year was a chipper one, urging us to remain calm, to carry on as usual but with a vigilant concern for our hygiene and public safety. Subsequent newsletters and emails had time- frames, in which promises were made about returning to campus and resuming the quality and capacity of learning. My most recent email from university included hacks to help with 'lockdown blues', etiquette around Zoom calls, and getting the 'most out of screen-to-screen learning'. My, how much can change in a year.

CHALLENGES OF STUDYING ONLINE

There have been considerable challenges as a student studying online during COVID-19. The lack of face-to-face interaction is notably difficult. Although it hasn't been the worst withdrawal for me personally, as so much of what I love about online learning is the autonomy, independence, and lack of small talk. During group-oriented tasks over the past year, however, the inability to meet and discuss in person, share ideas, and collaborate has been tricky. With the utmost respect to our teachers, the technical difficulties and general lack of proficiency has added to the stress and complexity. With that said, there could be more technical support from the university for staff and students to try and mitigate this as best as possible. In fairness, however, this is after all the university's first pandemic, so slack should be cut on all sides. We are all doing the best we can, and IT departments everywhere, no doubt, have never felt more acknowledged and loved. For me, the most difficult aspect has been the cancellation of practical clinic hours, and not being able to apply our theory in a practical setting. I was so looking forward to hours spent on campus in our student clinic, applying my knowledge of pharmacology and herbal medicine. I have subsequently missed out on seeing patients and learning how to prescribe and heal up close. This has all been postponed indefinitely.

THE PROS OF ONLINE LEARNING

On the other side of the coin there have been pros to online learning through this pandemic. For many of us working part-time or full-time, while also studying, it has allowed for us to learn from home. The pressure and expectation to be on campus during weekday hours, to meet the requirements for study, has dissipated and there is so much more flexibility and compassion around each person's circumstances. With the demand of part-time work, I initially would not have been able to study full-time this year as it would require days off work, however, when COVID-19 hit I went from working on-site to working from home, as well as scaling back my hours. This allowed me to maximise my time at home and up my study load, and I have been able to knock off nearly a year and a half of full-time study since the pandemic began.

Learning and working from home over this past year has required no travel time or public transport. In the time it would usually take me to travel to uni, attend a lecture and travel home, I have been able to squeeze in two lectures online. There has also been so much flexibility with online classes, picking a lecture that suits my week's schedule and being able to skip one if needed and catch up by watching the recording. Some lecturers have even been so lenient and have set up additional Zoom check-ins during the week to touch base to discuss content and provide extra support. This has been useful in the lead up to assessments, providing the opportunity to ask specific questions, as there isn't always time in the weekly lecture to ask individual questions in a sea of thirty voices, amid the echo of the same number of microphones and poor wi-fi connection.

These same teachers have also shown great compassion for the stress and anxiety that every one of us is feeling right now. A light has been shed on the fragility of mental health, where positivity and motivation and how our outside world can really affect our inside, becoming clearer. For the most part, it is our internal world and stress that creates pressure, and we have the outside world and its humdrum and monotony to balance things out. Whatever is going on with work, friends, kids, peers, partners, the outside world still has the same free-to-air commercials, the traffic is always bad, and the weather app looks far enough ahead that even the most anxious planner can see what the universe has in store. The outside world is the constant. Then COVID-19 happened. The outside world is no longer monotonous and safe, it is loud and depressing and the constant bearer of bad news. This has made our inside world so much harder to regulate and control. Having teachers and an institution acknowledge and support that has not only made learning feasible but also enjoyable throughout this difficult time.

THE PANDEMIC HAS SHAKEN EDUCATION TO ITS CORE

Learning is a right and a privilege that so many of us are lucky to experience, and for the most part, it is a challenging but predictable undertaking. The pandemic has shaken education to its core and changed the very way we connect, learn, and grow. The near future is not at all predictable, especially with COVID-19 still at large. Universities and providers have had to rise to the challenge and cater for students in a greater capacity than ever before. Learning - online learning, distance learning, blended learning, on-site learning - in all its forms has become far more student-centric and culture-centric than it has ever been. Providers have catered to students' needs amidst their socio-cultural context (a nation-wide lockdown) and the temperature of the wider world (a global pandemic). Perhaps the days are gone where the provider dictates how and when a student learns, and instead, a student has far more power to dictate how and where they wish to learn, encompassing personal context, health, and safety.

I have consistently opted for online learning in the past as it has proved more flexible and convenient, allowing me to plough through study while also living my life and fulfilling my work commitments. Despite the current situation, I am thoroughly enjoying online learning and appreciate the opportunity it has given me to get ahead. I am looking to the future and further study - another Masters, perhaps a Doctorate - and I will most certainly be looking for online study options. What will pique my interest is providers who have fared well during the pandemic and showed up for their students in a supportive, concrete way, where the quality of the course and integrity of learning have not and will not be compromised.

Online learning in the time of COVID-19 has been novel, in more than one sense; it is our first pandemic, and we are commemorating it in the written word. History in the making.

Lauren Whateley, graduate of both UNSW and UTS, currently studying Health Science at Torrens University online.

Facing reality: "Online Fatigue". Is this a real challenge for higher education?

Andy Wong

INTRODUCTION

Stanfort Academy, Faculty of Music (SFOM), was founded based on the concept of blended learning. The SFOM courses were taught with a combination of traditional on-campus sessions, online industry-expert masterclasses, and the signature Global Experience Workshops (GEX), where students experience intensive, real-life, practical-based learning. SFOM provides a unique proposition of global connectivity of award-winning industry experts through a series of online face to face (F2F) tutorials and a week-long GEX workshop as a capstone module at the end of every term. Due to the COVID-19 pandemic, the entire structure of blended learning turned into a full online face to face ZOOM conferencing mode.

EARLY STAGE

In March 2020, the COVID-19 pandemic shut down the economy of almost the entire world with all non-essential activities, including those of the higher education sector, made home-bound instantly. In Singapore, both the private and public education industries rushed into adopting a quick solution of "online learning", prematurely. Indeed, many private higher education institutions have the misconception that ZOOM conferencing is online learning.

A research article written by John R. Bryson & Lauren Andres (2020)[120] distinguishes between the development of Distance Learning Programmes and the rapid adoption of online learning. The article highlights the improvisation of online programme delivery that adopted a quick solution as a prescription to replace face to face classroom teaching, also known as the "buffering effect" (Villar & Miralles, 2020). In the case of many private higher education institutions in Singapore, the buffering effect was blatant where ZOOM classes replaced on-campus learning, period.

THE IMPACT OF THE "BUFFERING EFFECT."

Inevitably, students fell into the whirlpool of online fatigue. Whilst there are many causes of online fatigue, nonetheless, ZOOM conferencing is a prominent contributor. Schools that rely entirely on ZOOM, among other conferencing tools, such as, MS TEAM, GOOGLE MEET, and the like, would now face a declining student experience and motivation, including dropping out from school. At SFOM, our initial assessments were considered with the presumption of the unstable quality of video conferencing, such as, lousy audio quality due to latency, low video resolution, and bad internet connectivity.

Dr Jeffery Hall, however, in his book, "Relating Through Technology", writes, "ZOOM is exhausting, lonely, and if you are turning on the camera, you are seen as talking to yourself, and it can be disconcerting."[121] With a contrasting view in an empirical

[120] *https://www.tandfonline.com/doi/full/10.1080/03098265.2020.1807478*

[121] *https://www.insidehighered.com/digital-learning/blogs/online-trending-now/zoom-fatigue-what-we-have-learned*

study by C. Halupa[122] at East Texas Baptist University, United States, Halupa draws attention to the study of the prevalence of technological fatigue in the faculty. Overload usage of technology has led to a decrease in work performances as a result of the lack of social interaction, multi-tasking, and an overload of tasks - there is no direct evidence showing the correlation between learning and working experience. Fatigue caused by the overuse of technology, however, may directly impact both the physical and mental health of human beings.

MANAGING CHALLENGES

As a dean of the music faculty at Stanfort Academy, I came to embrace and recognise that the pandemic has been a learning curve and catalyst for building a much more robust and conducive online education. Before COVID-19, our focus was more on developing a virtual learning environment, incorporating the likes of Learning Management System (LMS), Mobile Applications, Online Learning Journals, and many more. Although such effort continues to evolve, our focus has since moved towards managing the learning experience by re-visiting the contents of the courses.

Concurrent to the Flex Model by Andrew West (2021)[123], face-to-face ZOOM sessions are now interactive and engaging as compared to "dry" lectures. Students are assigned missions to be completed before each lesson on the LMS in the form of quizzes and other software, including Rising Software for Theory and Aural studies. Online F2F/ZOOM classes are converted into discussion sessions or take place in the form of tuition.

EXPERIENTIAL LEARNING APPROACH

To reduce online fatigue, SFOM aims to balance the use of technological tools against the learner experience in the form of experiential learning. John M. Beckem and Michael Watkins (2012)

122 *https://www.researchgate.net/publication/329228644_TECHNOLOGY_FATIGUE_IN_FACULTY*

123 *https://www.ubss.edu.au/media/2716/what-is-meant-by-blended-learning.pdf*

write about the Immersive Learning Simulations (ILS), suggesting that the simulation of learning experience is best achieved through the combination of simulation, pedagogy, and fun - to create an engaging and behaviour-changing form of learning[124]. Adopting a similar model to the ILS, we aim to develop and stimulate learning through practical experiential learning, and increase the learning appetite with an array of activities created in the LMS.

Take our Western Music History course as an example. The course has been re-designed to stimulate the appreciation of music history through a series of interactive programmes. The course - which was once based on immense reading content - is now segmented into components of activities, including weekly listening quizzes where students listen, analyse, and explain the historical contents, as well as partake in topic presentations and the writing of short essays in a weekly forum writing session. The outcome has been positive, and students have developed an interest in the course. Learning based on experience is evidently suitable for online learning.

Live Music Performance courses such as ensemble and performance projects are now developed into producing performances online via social media applications, such as, Tik-Tok, Sessions and other online programmes. In addition to learning performance-related skills, students learn the necessary skills and gain knowledge to perform online, including studying the specifications of various online equipment, hardware and software, camera angles, lighting, and acoustic. Students are required to create Vlogs in place of journal writing for their performances and peer reviews. Concurrent to the ILS's personalized model[125], the simulated activities provide an engaging student-centred approach to learning (John M. B. & Michael. W, 2012). Such development strengthens students' communication and presentation skills and, at the same time, diverts attention and prevents online fatigue.

The effort does not end with the re-designing of courses or modules. It has indirectly encouraged tutors from all other courses to work together to find synergies and co-relation between them. Tutors have gained valuable insights into student performance which, in turn, contributes to maximising student learning

---

[124] *https://files.eric.ed.gov/fulltext/EJ1000091.pdf*

[125] *https://files.eric.ed.gov/fulltext/EJ1000091.pdf*

outcomes. The by-product of the chain of articulated work within the faculty has created the automated review and reflective practice of continuous improvement among faculty members. The Journal of Geography in Higher Education, written by Bryson, John R, et al. (2020), explains the natural shifting of the tutor's role in teaching online. The tutor now transforms from one role to another to better support students and the changing teaching environment. There is a shift from a teacher to facilitator, coordinator, encourager, and simulator to engage students in various ways and formats (Panigrahi et al., 2018)[126].

CONCLUSION

Before the pandemic, we could draw a clear line between Blended Learning, Massive Open Online Courses, and Hybrid Learning. COVID-19, to a certain extent, has erased the need to define the various online learning methods. Over the last eighteen months, students have been forced to face their computer screen extensively, and yet, a number of tutors have been unprepared to deliver the courses entirely online. Education institutions improvised lessons online without proper planning, neglecting the need to review their curriculum and pedagogy. As observed, the patterns of our students at SFOM demonstrated clearly unmistakable signs of declining interest and motivation, and, most importantly, of an increase in fatigue. Students showed signs of losing focus in almost every lesson toward the end of each term, and especially during the recent six months after a year of COVID-19. The faculty at SFOM has reviewed and refined how we deliver our courses, re-designing our course content with tutors coordinating and reviewing peer to peer to improve the processes and redefine their role. The question is whether such changes and improvements are sustainable.

Andy Wong, Dean of Stanfort Faculty of Music, and Co-founder of Hitmaker Global Academy, Singapore.

126 *https://www.tandfonline.com/doi/full/10.1080/03098265.2020.1807478*

Chapter

18

Blended learning: A new dimension for international students

Richard Xi

INTRODUCTION

Preparing a sustainable teaching/learning model for international students in the context of adapting to the 'new normal' of living with COVID-19 emerges as a new challenge for higher education providers. The unpredictable condition of travel restrictions, waiting periods and other unforeseeable uncertainty and changes for overseas students who choose Australia as their academic learning destination combine to present the necessary, if not urgent, requirement of designing a sustainable learning model to be delivered effectively within and beyond the pandemic. To meet this challenge, blended learning (bL) is suggested as the best possible learning model for international students. I support the point that bL can also be a new normal for both higher education institutions (HEIs) and international students in particular. It represents a new dimension in education which includes offering great flexibility and achieving an effective learning experience for international students in this 'new normal' context.

BLENDED LEARNING – ONE PLUS ONE GREATER THAN TWO

The definition of bL is well articulated among researchers, however, there is no universal consensus on the definition of this concept. Graham (2006)[127] defines blended learning simply as the combination of face-to-face instruction with computer-mediated instruction. Osguthorpe and Graham (2003, cited in Güzera and Canera, 2013)[128] suggest that "Blended learning combines face to face with distance delivery systems … but it's more than showing a page from a website on the classroom screen … those who use blended learning environments are trying to maximize the benefits of both face to face and online methods." Osguthorpe and Graham view blended learning as not just the simple combination of two different functional elements but emphasize the purpose of gaining the greatest benefit through the implementation of a new learning model.

Further, a research report from the Victorian Government Education Department[129] added that "… a blended learning approach provides innovative educational solutions through an effective mix of traditional classroom teaching with mobile learning and online activities." Driscoll (2002, cited in Hrastinski, 2019)[130] also argues that the point of blended learning is that it means different things to different people which "illustrates the untapped potential of blended learning."

The understanding of bL in a broader sense is that it does not just simply mix the different elements or models (for example, the face to face (F2F) delivery model and online delivery model) together as a new identity, it actually integrates them into a new model in a systematic way. "Blended learning is a way of combining the most positive aspects of traditional and distance learning and harnessing the valuable technology to provide a stimulating and effective

---

127 Graham, C. R. (2006). Blended learning systems: Definition, current trends and future directions. In C. J. Bonk & C. R. Graham (Eds.), The handbook of blended learning: Global perspectives, local designs (pp. 3–21). San Francisco: Pfeiffer.

128 *https://core.ac.uk/download/pdf/82476791.pdf*

129 *https://www.education.vic.gov.au/documents/about/research/blendedlearning.pdf*

130 *https://link.springer.com/article/10.1007/s11528-019-00375-5#Sec3*

environment for students." (Weil et al., 2014)[131]. The true meaning of bL should reflect Aristotle's philosophical belief: "the whole is greater than the sum of its parts." Regardless of the various definitions and opinions from different perspectives, the aim of blended learning is to maximise the benefit, which is generated from effective integration, for both the students and the institutions.

BLENDED LEARNING – ADVANTAGES AND BENEFITS

To get the best possible outcome from the implementation of the bL mode, a better understanding of the advantages and benefits of bL by international students and other stakeholders, such as their parents and agents, requires an effective and impressive communication strategy. Detailed information with an efficient and informed explanation of the advantages to students can compare well to the limited benefits they receive from either the face to face or online delivery model. As bL integrates the synchronous classroom and asynchronous online learning, it gives enormous flexibility to international students in managing their time and balancing their commitments to study and other duties - such as work and families - regardless of their geographical boundaries and time-zone differences. Given the flexibility that bL brings, it also strengthens students' budget power in better planning and controlling their study with a clearer cost-effective benefit. Thus, bL provides a tremendous benefit in terms of its convenience and flexibility.

With the accelerated development of technology, from the perspective of HEIs, there are always opportunities to update their information management facility and course delivery system to enrich and improve the teaching and learning environment to meet student needs. The ongoing improvement of course delivery quality and the overall learning experience not only helps to increase student satisfaction levels but also helps HEIs to gain the

[131] Weil, S., De Silva, T.-A. and Ward, M. (2014), "Blended learning in accounting: a New Zealand case", Meditari Accountancy Research, Vol. 22 No. 2, pp. 224-244

competitive advantage they need to survive within the industry in the context of the current crisis and an uncertain future.

BLENDED LEARNING – A NEW APPROACH GOES FORWARD AS 'NEW NORMAL'

We are experiencing and witnessing a paradigm shift within a short period of time - the dramatic, virtually 'overnight' change in the provision of higher education, away from the traditional F2F learning and teaching to off-campus online delivery. Nevertheless, in seeing the light at the end of the tunnel - after the articulation of the 'new normal' of living with COVID - HEIs need to prepare and plan to consider adopting blended learning as a new approach as the 'new normal' is not too far off. Notwithstanding the current exercise of state-wide lockdowns, it is reasonable to suggest that the 'new normal' indicates the worldwide border closures and travel constraints which stop international students coming into Australia may loosen in the near future, depending of course on the condition of a vaccination rate satisfying the government requirements.

Thanks to the rapid development of modern and advanced information and communication technology (ICT), the course delivery mode keeps evolving and it can provide more opportunity, flexibility, and variety to international students in their journey seeking knowledge, enjoying a positive learning experience, and benefiting from the high quality of Australian higher education. For international students, whether they are a current cohort or new, on-shore or off-shore, bL will configure itself effectively in the 'new normal' of living with COVID-19 by providing a combination of F2F and online learning course delivery, and itself will serve as a 'new normal' for HEIs and international students in the near future.

Richard Xi, Assistant Professor and Senior Postgraduate Co-ordinator, UBSS.

Are they there?

Stephen JK Parker

INTRODUCTION

Everything is prepared, slides are ready, the friendly welcome message has been added to the chat window, and you've remembered to press the record button. It's time to turn on the video, open your mic and announce with confidence "Welcome to this week's online lecture".

Silence…………..and the lyrics from Pink Floyd's "Is there anybody out there?" start echoing in your head.

I am relatively new to the world of academic teaching (4+ years). However, my 30+ years of commercial experience has been focused on connecting innovative technology with strategic business value and this has involved teaching throughout. A key part of this journey has involved being "on stage", both physically and virtually, with audiences from tens to thousands.

My goal for this article is to share the experiences I have gained from both these worlds and hopefully make the song quieter.

I do not expect what I share below to create blinding revelations, but maybe it will give you confidence, by re-enforcing what you are doing already or remind you of things to try again.

WHAT DO WE MEAN BY "ARE THEY THERE?"

Before we dive into solutions let us check what we mean by "Are they there?". At its simplest we can consider this from two perspectives, are the students *physically present* and separately are the *intellectually present.*

Physically Present

Testing physical presence is relatively easy. We used to ask students to swipe into the lecture room, and now we can see if they have logged into the online lecture room. The value of this limited as students have always and will continue to, game the system.

However, there are compliance issues that need to be considered, whether these be driven by internal or external standards. For example, education regulators, especially in relation to overseas students. The "hard evidence" of physical presence is a key part of these compliance requirements.

Intellectually Present

This is far more difficult to assess. In the online context even the notion of where to consider the intellectual engagement changes. With course assets, lecture recordings et al being available at any time, does the measurement occur during the narrow window of the lecture or should we measure the time and nature of the students ongoing access to the course assets?

Even when face-to-face and therefore physically present there are a range of intellectually present states – from fully engaged, asking, and responding to questions, through states of distraction, all the way to asleep at the back of the room. However, at least when face-to-face, you can read the room and see which students are not engaged and can make efforts to change this (even if only to give them a pillow so they are comfortable).

One of the great learning opportunities in my career was IBM Sales School. At one of the residential parts of the year long course, the senior instructor approached me at the bar and the following conversation occurred:

"Stephen, you are possibly the most frustrating student I have ever taught."

With concern, I asked *"Why so?"*

With a smile he answered, *"I would swear you were asleep in today's class, so I asked you the most challenging question I could think of, and you just opened your eyes and gave the perfect answer, referencing specific content from the class."*

Smiling in return I said *"Not everyone listens with their eyes open"*

We all have our own approaches to learning. There have been multiple attempts to codify these different "Learning Styles"[132], one popular one being the VARK model (Visual, Auditory, Reading/writing, Kinesthetic). However, the simplistic application of these models, with each student assigned a dominant style is being questioned[133]

For example, during lectures some students will want to clarify points immediately, whilst others although "silent" may be taking notes to review later. Also, not all engagement adds value and can be frustrating to fellow students. For example, addressing points covered in previous lectures where the student did not attend and has failed to review the online materials and available recording. If asking questions is the measure of engagement, then be carefully what you wish for, lectures may never end.

POSSIBLE SOLUTIONS

Enforced Video

For small groups this works, especially for personal, mentoring or group project activities, where the intimacy of visual interaction can be used. For larger classes it is not practical for the lecturer to "check" all 50+ students, all the time, but selectively asking a student to activate the video can add value.

[132] *https://www.education.vic.gov.au/documents/childhood/professionals/support/egsls.pdf*
[133] *https://www.scientificamerican.com/article/the-problem-with-learning-styles/*

As an example, getting the students to be "2-minute guest presenters", where they provide a short summary of research they have carried out as part of one of their personal assessments/projects.

There are other technical and social challenges associated with enforcing video, such as limitations in the student's bandwidth and equipment or their personal situation/environment. This digital divide has been highlighted during COVID where disadvantaged students have been even further disadvantaged during online learning[134]. We must also remember that not everywhere has the same stable environment, whether that be infrastructure, social, political, or even weather conditions.

I have had (verified) apologies for absence from students due to typhoons, and both planned and unplanned blackouts taking out infrastructure for days.

Enforcing video and hence recorded evidence of presence, has value where compliance of "physical" attendance is essential, but this is more about post lecture "audit" than in-lecture value.

My experience is that video should be used selectively, where it clearly enhances the learning engagement between the student, their fellow students, and the lecturer.

Real time engagement Sentiment

The use of real time eye tracking in the automotive industry is growing rapidly, largely driven by safety[135] and monitoring in the "driver assisted" levels of the Self-Driving taxonomy[136]. Also, keyboard and screen monitoring software has had a boost due to the desire for management to monitor the activity of staff working remotely due to COVID-19. These technologies are starting to appear as add-ons to collaboration and learning management platforms, with AI being used to derive engagement sentiment.

There is push back from a privacy perspective[137] but maybe more fundamentally is the question as to whether these are valid

134 *https://www.school-news.com.au/news/digital-divide-impacts-vulnerable-students/*
135 *https://www.motor.com/magazine-summary/eye-on-electronics-november-2019/*
136 *https://en.wikipedia.org/wiki/Self-driving_car*
137 *https://www.abc.net.au/news/2020-10-16/work-from-home-tracking-software-monitoring/12766020*

measures of engagement in either a commercial or academic environment. Does looking away from the camera/screen mean you are not thinking? Does using the keyboard indicate real work or simply gaming the software?

One use case that does appear to have valid benefits is in proctored examinations. We accepted in the physical world that there would be invigilators during examinations, so why not online? Again, this can be driven by the need for compliance, with some external bodies requiring exams to be proctored for them to be recognised/accepted.

Analysis of engagement with learning Assets

A potentially more powerful measure of sentiment would be the student's engagement with the digital assets provided as part of the course.

- What has been their activity on the learning platform (Moodle etc)?
- Have they watched lecture recordings and if so, how often and for how long?
- Who has been actively communicating on the Group Project collaboration platform?

Whilst much of the data to support this sentiment analysis exists, it is rarely turned into information that can be *easily* used by the lecturer. This could be used to support those that are not engaged, or to identify areas where multiple students are re-reading/watching the same content, possibly indicating topics that need to be covered again in a future lecture.

Some platforms such as Microsoft Teams offer these engagement insights within the Education tailored version of their product[138].

The power of the Chat Window

To re-engage with the students after breaks, even though I am confident that the video and mic are working, I ask "can you see and hear me?", with a challenge to be the quickest to respond in

138 *https://docs.microsoft.com/en-us/microsoftteams/class-insights*

the chat window and a minimum of two responses required to progress.

I use the same approach at regular intervals, when asking if anyone has questions, with a simple emoji being an acceptable response. Emoji's offer various benefits over a written response:

- It is quicker for the student to respond
- I can scan/glance a 👍 much quicker than reading
- There is sentiment built in – with a 👍 being OK, but a 😀 being OK and happy.
- Students can also share their personality 😎

I have found that this gamification plus a personal thank you to each student who responds also increases the speed and quantity of responses.

The chat window also provides the power to not answer immediately, but to acknowledge, and respond later. This is especially true of the private chat window, allowing the student the safety of asking questions without the public glare and for the lecturer to respect their privacy and respond either in generic terms or directly when convenient.

Gamification and Non-Assessed Quizzes

Asking questions to test engagement during lectures, typically results in the usual suspects responding. This means that the remaining students are left in "receiving" mode for the entire lecture.

Quizzes can provide a powerful way to switch the student's mode from "receiving" to "thinking". However, formal, assessed quizzes are both complex to administer (fairness) and if used too often can leave the student with a sense of being over-assessed.

An approach I have used, is to use non-assessed quizzes based on the following principles:

- Anonymous – having a go is more important than being right. Thinking mode will increase retention even if you are wrong
- Different styles – opinion based, research based, gamified with the quickest right answer and a leader board
- Typically, 3 per lecture and aligned to short breaks (see "Power of the Chat Window" above)
- Fun can be introduced into the questions without the concern for academic integrity – engagement is more important
- A personalised post quiz discussion based on the responses from the students

> The student feedback of me calling the real time responses to quizzes as if they were a horse race has been very positive.

JUST ACCEPT THEY MAY NOT BE "THERE"

This may seem heretical, but in the commercial world this is just a given. People sign up for webinars and fail to attend all the time. Because of this there is conscious planning for low or even no attendance. Questions can be fed into the chat window by the moderator to stimulate those who have attended. "Questions from the audience" are pre-prepared in case there are no attendee questions in the Q&A session at the end. Prizes are offered to attendees who stay to the end, with questions based on content from the webinar.

So why do they do this?

- Because they know in advance that attendance rates are extremely variable
- So, they get contact information of people who were at least interested enough to register
- To gain a clear indication of serious interest from those who did attend

- As a mechanism to create digital artifacts (the recorded webinar, associated materials, flyers, PowerPoints et al) that can be used both for follow up with those who registered, and for use in ongoing activities and campaigns.

The critical aspect is that the mindset is not driven by compliance and enforced attendance at the live event, but rather about ongoing engagement with a focus on those who did attend, and the creation of assets for trailing engagement with the rest.

CONCLUSION

Teaching, like many other sectors has been forced to undergo radical transformation during the COVID-19 pandemic, with a major aspect of this being a shift to online and remote engagement. Will all these changes be retained as is? In many ways I hope not.

Surely this is only the "end of the beginning", with so many areas that we can learn from and therefore still improve. I am excited by the opportunities ahead as we explore this new era of hybrid, blended and online learning.

Stephen JK Parker, Assistant Professor, Specialising in Innovation and Entrepreneurship, Fellow of the UBSS Centre for Entrepreneurship

Compilation of References

ID	Reference	Ch
1	www.toyota.com.au/Kluger	1
2	https://www.theguardian.com/australia-news/2021/jun/20/universities-ramping-up-hybrid-learning-means-double-the-work-for-same-pay-staff-say	1
3	https://blog.highereducationwhisperer.com/2021/06/teaching-hybrid-mode-in-dual-delivery.html	1
4	https://www.monash.edu/learning-teaching/teaching-resources/search/user-guides/hybrid-teaching-models	1
5	https://www.ted.com/watch/tedx-talks	1
6	https://www.campusreview.com.au/2021/06/what-the-lack-of-onshore-international-students-in-2021-means-for-2022/	1
7	https://www.forbes.com/sites/brandonbusteed/2021/05/02/pandemic-to-permanent-11-lasting-changes-to-higher-education/?sh=137189bb452f	1
8	https://www.ubss.edu.au/	1
9	Orey, M (2002). One year of online blended learning: Lessons learned. Paper presented at the Annual Meeting of the Eastern Educational Research Association, Sarasota, FL	2
10	Driscoll, M (2002). Blended Learning: Let's get beyond the hype. eLearning, 54.	2
11	Reay, J (2001). Blended Learning - a fusion for the future. Knowledge Management Review, 4(3), 6.	2
12	Bonk, C and Graham, C (Eds.). (2006). Handbook of Blended Learning: Global Perspectives, Local Designs. San Francisco, CA: Pfeiffer Publishing.	2
13	Bonk, C and Graham, C (Eds.). (2006). Handbook of Blended Learning: Global Perspectives, Local Designs. San Francisco, CA: Pfeiffer Publishing.	2
14	Horn, M and Staker. H (2014) Blended: Using Disruptive Innovation to Improve Schools. San Francisco, CA: Jossey-Bass, 2014.	2

ID	Reference	Ch
15	McCann, J (2020) Is A Blended Office Model The Future Of Work? https://www.forbes.com/sites/forbesbusinesscouncil/2020/10/20/is-a-blended-office-model-the-future-of-work/?sh=1621091002ea	2
16	Johnson E (2021) Digital learning is real-world learning. That's why blended on-campus and online study is best, https://theconversation.com/digital-learning-is-real-world-learning-thats-why-blended-on-campus-and-online-study-is-best-163002	2
17	https://adamasuniversity.ac.in/a-brief-history-of-online-education/	3
18	Carey, K. (2020). Is everybody ready for the big migration to online college? Actually, no. The New York Times. https://www.nytimes.com	3
19	https://news.harvard.edu/gazette/story/2013/04/online-learning-its-different/	3
20	https://www.edweek.org/technology/opinion-how-effective-is-online-learning-what-the-research-does-and-doesnt-tell-us/2020/03	3
21	Liyang Song, Enrise S, Singleton, Jannette R, Hill, Myung Hwa Koh (2004) Improving Online Learning: Student perceptions of useful and Challenging characteristics, The Internet and Higher Education, 7(1): 59-70	3
22	Mayleen Dorcas B Castro and Gilbert M Tumibay (2021) A literature Review: Efficacy of online learning courses for higher education institution using meta-analysis, Education and Information technologies, 26, 1367-1385.	3
23	Sim, Sandra Phek-Lin; Sim, Hannah Phek-Khiok; Quah, Cheng-Sim (2020) Online Learning: A Post COVID-19 Alternative Pedagogy for University Students, Asian Journal of University Education, 16(4), 137-151	3
24	Yuk MingTang, Pen Chung Chen, Kris M.Y.Law, C.H.Wu, cYui-yipLau, Jieqi Guan, Dan He, G.T.S.Ho (2021) Comparative analysis of Student's live online learning readiness during the coronavirus (COVID-19) pandemic in the higher education sector, Computers & Education, 168, https://doi.org/10.1016/j.compedu.2021.10421	3
25	https://www.brandonhall.com/blogs/tag/e-learning/	3
26	https://news.harvard.edu/gazette/story/2013/04/online-learning-its-different/	3

ID	Reference	Ch
27	https://www.ibm.com/blogs/think/2020/03/pandemic-impacts-millions-of-students-how-digital-learning-can-help/	3
28	https://www.forbes.com/sites/paycom/2017/02/14/learning-management-systems-101-rethinking-your-approach-to-employee-training/?sh=d63db37755bc	3
29	https://www3.open.ac.uk/events/3/2005331_47403_o1.pdf	3
30	https://acquire.cqu.edu.au/articles/report/Projects_iCon_and_Uptech_Creating_infrastructure_for_the_virtual_Conservatorium/13429160	4
31	https://www.smartbrief.com/original/2018/08/whats-old-new-again	4
32	https://link.springer.com/article/10.1007/s10639-021-10612-1	4
33	https://onlineinnovationsjournal.com/streams/visual-and-performing-arts/63209b3a0ef5fedf.html	4
34	https://www.campusreview.com.au/2020/09/full-marks-for-educators-the-digital-convicts-of-covid-19/	4
35	https://www.campusreview.com.au/2021/07/new-research-looks-at-how-performing-arts-teachers-and-students-are-coping-in-a-time-of-remote-learning/	4
36	https://musescore.org/en/download	4
37	https://link.springer.com/article/10.1007/s10758-020-09477-z	4
38	https://www.risingsoftware.com/auralia	4
39	GILLETT-SWAN, Jenna. The Challenges of Online Learning: Supporting and Engaging the Isolated Learner. Journal of Learning Design, [S.l.], v. 10, n. 1, p. 20-30, jan. 2017. ISSN 1832-8342. Available at: https://www.jld.edu.au/article/view/293/269	5
40	Those higher education institutions who are not self-accrediting	5
41	https://ihea.edu.au/news/independent-higher-education-providers-best-in-country-qilt-results/ accessed 27 July 2021	5
42	https://blog.hubspot.com/marketing/productivity-tips-working-from-home accessed 29 July 2021	5
43	https://www.nsw.gov.au/covid-19/safe-workplaces/workers/working-from-home accessed 29 July 2021	5
44	https://www.hrmonline.com.au/employment-law/family-domestic-violence-working-from-home/ accessed 29 July 2021	5
45	https://www.ubss.edu.au/articles/2021/may/online-teaching-a-tale-of-two-institutions/	5

ID	Reference	Ch
46	https://www.ubss.edu.au/articles/2021/may/online-teaching-a-tale-of-two-institutions/	5
47	https://www.ubss.edu.au/media/2670/understanding-hybrid-delivery.pdf	5
48	https://www.ubss.edu.au/media/2670/understanding-hybrid-delivery.pdf	5
49	https://www.ubss.edu.au/media/2695/the-efficacy-of-online-studies.pdf	5
50	https://internationaleducation.gov.au/regulatory-information/Education-Services-for-Overseas-Students-ESOS-Legislative-Framework/National-Code/Pages/default.aspx	6
51	https://www.ubss.edu.au/media/2716/what-is-meant-by-blended-learning.pdf	6
52	https://www.ubss.edu.au/media/2695/the-efficacy-of-online-studies.pdf	6
53	https://www.ubss.edu.au/media/2670/understanding-hybrid-delivery.pdf	6
54	http://thirdway.imgix.net/pdfs/one-year-later-covid-19s-impact-on-current-and-future-college-students.pdf	6
55	Berger J. and Milkman K. L. (2012) What makes online content Viral? Journal of Marketing Research, Vol. XLIX, 192 –205. https://doi.org/10.1509/jmr.10.0353	7
56	https://www.forbes.com/sites/jasonbloomberg/2018/04/29/digitization-digitalization-and-digital-transformation-confuse-them-at-your-peril/?sh=fb2466a2f2c7	7
57	https://online.osu.edu/resources/learn/whats-difference-between-asynchronous-and-synchronous-learning	7
58	https://www.udemy.com/course/how-to-write-the-best-online-content/	7
59	https://www.tandfonline.com/doi/citedby/10.1080/13562517.2021.1872527?scroll=top&needAccess=true	7
60	Fearnley, Marissa R.; Amora, Johnny T. (2020), Learning Management System Adoption in Higher Education Using the Extended Technology Acceptance Model, IAFOR Journal of Education, 8(2), 89-106.	7
61	https://link.springer.com/content/pdf/10.1007/s10758-020-09475-1.pdf	7
62	https://eric.ed.gov/?id=EJ1277763	7

ID	Reference	Ch
63	https://www.teacheracademy.eu/blog/game-based-learning/	7
64	https://www.ncbi.nlm.nih.gov/pmc/articles/PMC2966567/	7
65	Jee Hyun Lee, Eunkyoung Yang, Zhong Yuan Sun. (2021) Using an Immersive Virtual Reality Design Tool to Support Cognitive Action and Creativity: Educational Insights from Fashion Designers. The Design Journal 24:4, pages 503-524.	7
66	Aldous Huxley wrote Brave New World in 1932. It foreshadowed a number of social and scientific developments (including invitro fertilisation, genetic cloning, helicopters and genetically modified babies, as well as antidepressants and fascism) before they became realities.	8
67	F.O. Ramirez & J. Boli, (1987). The political construction of mass schooling: European origins and worldwide institutionalization. F.O. Ramirez & J. Boli (1987). Sociology of education, 1987–JSTOR https://www.jstor.org/stable/2112615	8
68	Conor King (2021). Education Follows the Big Drivers. Farewell Address to the ATN, reported in CMM, 28th July 2021	8
69	Half of UK university students think degree is poor value for money. Results from The Higher Education Policy Group Thinktank, Student Survey. Rachel Hall, The Guardian, UK. 21 6 2021	8
70	Student satisfaction in Australian universities drops to an all-time low. Editorial, The Guardian, Australia. 21/03/2021	8
71	'Too many graduates, too few jobs…' The Australian, 26th July 2020	8
72	Althusser, Louis (2014) On the Reproduction of Capitalism: Ideology and Ideological State Apparatuses. Verso UK	8
73	Universities Australia, 3rd February 2021	8
74	Mienczakowski, J. & Whateley, G. Ranking addiction: Time to rethink the habit? Campus Review, 16th Feb 2021	8
75	Tim Dodd HE Editor. (The Australian July 17-18, 2021)	8
76	ICEF Monitor, International Survey of education agents reveals optimism (2021)	9
77	Hurley, P. (2020) Coronavirus and International Students	9
78	Australian Bureau of Statistics. 2019-2020	9
79	RBA Bulletin, December 2020	9
80	Hurley, P. (2020) Coronavirus, and the International Student	9

ID	Reference	Ch
81	Hurley, P. (2020) International students vital to the coronavirus recovery	9
82	Hurley, P. (2020) International students vital to the coronavirus recovery	9
83	Oanh (Olena) Thi Kim Nguyen & Varsha Devi Balakrishnan (2020) International students in Australia – during and after COVID-19, Higher Education Research & Development	9
84	International Education. International students and their mental health and physical safety, p.10	9
85	World Economic Forum, The Covid-19 has changed education forever. This is how. April 2020	9
86	Online Education: Worldwide Status, Challenges, Trends, and Implications	9
87	National Education Association, Overview Hybrid Learning Models, 2021	9
88	Tertiary Education and Quality Standards Agency, November 2020	9
89	Joint Media Release, The Hon Alan Tudge MP, July 2020	9
90	https://www.ubss.edu.au/media/2760/alternate-delivery-modes-for-international-students.pdf accessed 3 August 2021	10
91	https://www.ubss.edu.au/articles/2021/may/online-teaching-a-tale-of-two-institutions/ accessed 3 August 2021	10
92	https://www.ubss.edu.au/media/1824/transition-to-online-teaching-and-learning-at-ubss-2020.pdf accessed 4 August 2021	10
93	https://www.ubss.edu.au/media/2754/online-learning-and-the-organisation.pdf accessed 3 August 2021	10
94	https://www.abc.net.au/news/2019-10-11/murdoch-university-sues-four-corners-whistleblower/11591520 accessed 3 August 2021	10
95	https://www.dese.gov.au/esos-framework accessed 3 August 2021	10
96	https://www.dese.gov.au/esos-framework/resources/standard-8-overseas-student-visa-requirements	10
97	https://www.dese.gov.au/esos-framework/resources/standard-3-formalisation-enrolment-and-written-agreements see Standard 3.	10
98	https://www.education.vic.gov.au/school/students/beyond/Pages/dutiesofemployers.aspx accessed 4 August 2021	10

ID	Reference	Ch
99	Knowles, M., Holton, E., and Swanson, R., The Adult Learner – The Definitive Classic in Adult Education and Human Resource Development, 5 ed 1998, Butterworth-Heinemann, Woburn, MA, USA	11
100	www.UBSS.edu.au	11
101	Bonk, C and Graham, C (Eds.). (2006). Handbook of blended learning: Global Perspectives, local designs. San Francisco, CA: Pfeiffer Publishing	11
102	https://www.cybintsolutions.com/3-benefits-of-hybrid-learning/	12
103	https://clas.ucdenver.edu/working-remotely/faculty/pedagogy-time-disruption/advantages-and-disadvantages-synchronous-and-asynchronous-teaching	12
104	https://teaching.washington.edu/topics/engaging-students-in-learning/	12
105	https://www.ubss.edu.au/never-lose-the-moment/	12
106	https://www.blackboard.com/en-apac/teaching-learning/collaboration-web-conferencing/blackboard-collaborate	12
107	https://medium.com/@Slidoapp/why-and-how-to-organize-fireside-chats-at-your-event-74ee55e90334	12
108	https://www.ted.com/watch/tedx-talks	12
109	https://hbsp.harvard.edu/inspiring-minds/engaging-students-on-the-first-day-and-every-day	12
110	https://www.ubss.edu.au/media/2760/alternate-delivery-modes-for-international-students.pdf	13
111	https://www.ubss.edu.au/media/2759/future-experience.pdf	13
112	https://www.ubss.edu.au/media/2695/the-efficacy-of-online-studies.pdf	13
113	https://www.ubss.edu.au/media/2761/impact-of-coronavirus.pdf	13
114	https://www.ubss.edu.au/media/2761/impact-of-coronavirus.pdf	13
115	Handel, M., Stephan, M, Glaser-Zikuda, M., Kopp, B., Bedenlier, S. & Ziegler, A. (2020). Digital readiness and its effects on higher education students' socio-emotional perceptions in the context of the COVID-19 pandemic. https://www.tandfonline.com/doi/full/10.1080/15391523.2020.1846147	14

ID	Reference	Ch
116	Alsadoon, H. (2021). Challenges of deploying online exams. https://lumenpublishing.com/journals/index.php/rrem/article/download/3439/2916/13320	14
117	Chanda, A. (2021). The Efficacy of Online Studies: Addressing the Student Dilemma. https://www.ubss.edu.au/media/2695/the-efficacy-of-online-studies.pdf	14
118	https://elmlearning.com/blended-learning-everything-need-know/	15
119	https://www.edgepointlearning.com/blog/benefits-of-blended-learning/	15
120	https://www.tandfonline.com/doi/full/10.1080/03098265.2020.1807478	17
121	https://www.insidehighered.com/digital-learning/blogs/online-trending-now/zoom-fatigue-what-we-have-learned	17
122	https://www.researchgate.net/publication/329228644_TECHNOLOGY_FATIGUE_IN_FACULTY	17
123	https://www.ubss.edu.au/media/2716/what-is-meant-by-blended-learning.pdf	17
124	https://files.eric.ed.gov/fulltext/EJ1000091.pdf	17
125	https://files.eric.ed.gov/fulltext/EJ1000091.pdf	17
126	https://www.tandfonline.com/doi/full/10.1080/03098265.2020.1807478	17
127	Graham, C. R. (2006). Blended learning systems: Definition, current trends and future directions. In C. J. Bonk & C. R. Graham (Eds.), The handbook of blended learning: Global perspectives, local designs (pp. 3–21). San Francisco: Pfeiffer.	18
128	https://core.ac.uk/download/pdf/82476791.pdf	18
129	https://www.education.vic.gov.au/documents/about/research/blendedlearning.pdf	18
130	https://link.springer.com/article/10.1007/s11528-019-00375-5#Sec3	18
131	Weil, S., De Silva, T.-A. and Ward, M. (2014), "Blended learning in accounting: a New Zealand case", Meditari Accountancy Research, Vol. 22 No. 2, pp. 224-244	18
132	https://www.education.vic.gov.au/documents/childhood/professionals/support/egsls.pdf	19
133	https://www.scientificamerican.com/article/the-problem-with-learning-styles/	19

ID	Reference	Ch
134	https://www.school-news.com.au/news/digital-divide-impacts-vulnerable-students/	19
135	https://www.motor.com/magazine-summary/eye-on-electronics-november-2019/	19
136	https://en.wikipedia.org/wiki/Self-driving_car	19
137	https://www.abc.net.au/news/2020-10-16/work-from-home-tracking-software-monitoring/12766020	19
138	https://docs.microsoft.com/en-us/microsoftteams/class-insights	19

Notes pages

We hope that this book has inspired you and that you have already scribbled your thoughts all over it. However, if you have ideas that need a little more space then please use these notes pages.

Notes pages

www.ingramcontent.com/pod-product-compliance
Lightning Source LLC
LaVergne TN
LVHW010939100826
845153LV00001B/95

* 9 7 8 1 9 0 7 4 5 3 3 1 1 *